A CONFLICT OF IDEAS
IN THE
LATE ROMAN EMPIRE

A CONFLICT OF IDEAS
IN THE
LATE ROMAN EMPIRE

The Clash between the
Senate and Valentinian I

BY

ANDREW ALFÖLDI

TRANSLATED BY

HAROLD MATTINGLY

GREENWOOD PRESS, PUBLISHERS
WESTPORT, CONNECTICUT

Library of Congress Cataloging in Publication Data

Alföldi, András, 1895-
  A conflict of ideas in the late Roman Empire.

    Reprint of the ed. published by the Clarendon Press,
Oxford.
    Includes bibliographical references and index.
    1. Valentinianus I, Emperor of Rome, 321-375.
2. Rome. Senate. 3. Rome--History--Vanentinianus I,
364-375. 4. Persecution--Early church, ca. 30-600.
I. Title.
[DG323.A33 1979b]   937'.6   78-26781
ISBN 0-313-20836-0

Reprinted in 1979 by Greenwood Press, Inc.
51 Riverside Avenue, Westport, CT 06880

Printed in the United States of America

10 9 8 7 6 5 4 3 2 1

FOREWORD

ANYONE who has travelled down the Danube to Hungary by steamer will probably remember the romantic beauty of the country above Budapest and the picturesque ruined castle of Visegrád. The river, flowing from west to east, here takes a sudden, sharp turn to the south. Behind this abrupt turn of the mighty river, which was once the boundary of the Roman world, the high ridge of the mountain of Dobogókő commands the whole district. The climber sees at his feet towards the south the great city with its millions. To the north-east he has a clear view of the Ipoly flowing into the Danube, like the Roman watchmen in old days who, from this point of vantage, observed the unruly Sarmatians on the farther bank and the mustering of the raiding-parties of the German Quadi. On the very top of the mountain the foundations of a Roman watch-tower have been found, and the paved road which led up to it can still be used. And farther up on the fruitful plain of the Ipoly were once massed those German peoples who won deliverance from the yoke of the Huns at the fateful battle for the lordship of the Danube lands. Somewhat farther to the west the Danube receives the waters of the Garam, on the banks of which the philosopher Emperor, Marcus Aurelius, with the roar of the battle with wild barbarians raging round him, wrote down his *Meditations*. And, to the north of Dobogókő, one can see the dome of the Basilica of Esztergom gleaming; whilst behind this sanctuary, where Western Christianity has been at home for a thousand years, the outlines of the Carpathians appear, in fine weather, in the far distance. . . . But the eye of the historian, I believe, can cover even longer distances from this viewpoint. At the place where East and West part, set, too, between north and south, he gains from this mountain a survey of the whole of the lost Roman Empire.

It was in the healthful loneliness of this mountain, with its girdle of woods, that this book was written in the last years of the Second World War. Every evening, along the path by our house, that they knew from of old, strings of stags would run past to drink at the pool hard by. During the day we saw the great English and American aeroplanes passing in their hundreds: we looked to them for deliverance, although they were bombarding our city.

Even before the German General Staff had commandeered our house, before the mountain, my favourite place of pilgrimage in childhood, had changed hands, time and time again, between the armies of Hitler and Stalin, before we had begun to drag out our precarious existence in the cellars of the University of Budapest during the endless months of the siege, this book had been completed.[1] But, under the distressful circumstances, under the strain, the fearful strain of my certainty of the coming catastrophe, I could never have got through my task but for the moral support and physical care that my wife lavished on me. In the hour of supreme danger, released by that very danger, amazing energies and moral qualities blossomed in this wife of mine, at the very moment when I myself was most broken down. I decided at the time to dedicate this little book, the making of which is so largely due to her, as a small token to her of the thirty years in which we have shared our joys and sorrows.

The next volume will append to the trials for magic under Valentinian the tale of the strange paths that the ancient world followed in the mists of magic. Now that I have found a second home in free Switzerland I hope, in no long time, to be able to produce it; the other links of this chain of studies shall follow—if God will.

My honoured friend, Harold Mattingly, has helped me during publication—to him I owe the fine style and clear formulation of the English text; I owe much also to the skilled staff of the Clarendon Press. With thanks to them in my heart, I send my book on its way with the words of Ovid:

> vade liber, verbisque meis loca grata saluta!
> contingam certe, quo licet, illa pede.

BERNE

August 1948

---

[1] A summary of the results has been given in a lecture on the Sorbonne, May 1946, published in the *Revue d'Histoire Comparée*, N.S. iii, 1946, under the title 'Valentinien Ier, le dernier des grands Pannoniens'.

CONTENTS

INTRODUCTION

IN an earlier volume we followed the course of the fight, waged from A.D. 312 onwards, by the aristocracy of the city of Rome in defence of its ancient conceptions of religion and ethics against the new Christian Government. It was astonishing to observe the ripe political wisdom, the diplomatic skill, worthy of a brilliant past, and the impressive moral dignity with which a society, often described by modern scholars as one of decadent, worthless parasites, defended the sacred traditions of their ancestors.

But, when we turn our attention to the frictions which soon after the death of Julian began between the new holder of power and the Senate, the latest scions of the great old families no longer appear in so favourable a light. They are no longer inspired by pure patriotism, but by selfish class-interest. Their real concern is for the unjustifiable privileges that they enjoyed at law, and they are furious at losing their titbits. For Valentinian I left the pagan cults of Rome in peace and, unlike his predecessors, only persecuted magic and witchcraft with their attendant absurdities. If the defenders of the old Roman traditions came into bitter conflict with him, they in their opposition to him were not entirely innocent.

Our sources, it is true, give a different view of the fight and look for the blame simply and solely in the Emperor and his entourage, and modern scholars follow them. If, then, we mean to obtain a clear view, we must above all try to get in the right focus the personality and political aims of Valentinian and the activities of the intimates who carried them out, and against them we must set the endeavours of the great senatorial landowners.

Our conclusion may be set out in advance. Deep, very deep in the past lay events and prejudices that raised an impassable barrier between the two opposed parties. Two worlds stand confronted, strange and unintelligible to one another. On the one side is the Emperor, with his beloved companions in arms, his courtiers from Illyricum and other provinces, and others who are his blind tools. On the other side stand the descendants of the great Roman families, an oligarchy of birth and wealth at once. Neither group can realize the creative power or the wide political and historical importance of the other ; but both fully comprehend the very real weaknesses of their rivals. There was a gulf here which the omnipotence of the Late Empire was quite unable to bridge, or even to understand. We must now try to discover what profit and loss to the world-State and, indirectly, to its late posterity, was to result from these two worlds of thought.

I

THE LAST OF THE GREAT PANNONIAN EMPERORS

THE figure of Valentinian I has been projected by the historians of the senatorial aristocracy that opposed him into a distorting mirror. We shall show later in detail that the group of society whose ideas he brought with him to the throne had not the control of any similar organ of publicity to echo its thoughts and plans and to support its policy. Ammianus Marcellinus, the great historian of the fourth century, whose work is our main source for judging the reign of our Emperor, actually drew his picture of the rule of Valentinian from the work of a Roman of high rank: I mean, Nicomachus Flavianus, who took an active part in the fight with Valentinian.[1] Ammianus, then, drew on a source itself hostile to Valentinian; and his own style, with its high colouring, its more than Tacitean bitterness, and its passion for superlatives, was made to exaggerate the convictions from which it set out. We must never forget that for Ammianus, however honourable and able he might be, history did not appear as a science but as an art. The rhetorical culture of the age which absorbed into itself all other aims required that it should be a special kind of oratory.[2] That is why the literary fashion of the age, artificial, florid, and capricious in its choice of words, had free play in the work of Ammianus. With it went the theatrical trick of exploiting exciting situations. His emotional narrative is like a Late Baroque altar, swarming with grotesque details. Besides this strong underlying bias Ammianus was also influenced by a certain personal antipathy. He had been devoted, body and soul, to Julian, and this made him intolerant of the two brothers to whom the personality and policy of Julian were so alien.[3] Over and above this

[1] See Note 1, p. 128.

[2] Cf. W. Ensslin, *Zur Geschichtsschreibung und Weltanschauung des Ammianus Marcellinus*, iii, 1923–39; E. A. Thompson, *The Historical Work of Ammianus Marcellinus*, 1947, 126. I could not yet consult the book of M. L. W. Laistner, *The Greater Roman Historians* (Sather Classical Lectures for 1947).

[3] We feel this, for example, in xxvi. 10. 8: 'Fronimius . . . inclementius in

he stood himself for a while in danger through the prosecutions
for magic ordered by Valens in the East, on occasion of a conspiracy.[1]

But even more serious confusion is occasioned by Ammianus'
curious method of passing judgement, which has not been sufficiently noticed by modern scholars. In describing the history
of the individual Emperors he records their good and bad qualities apart and does not even try to reconcile those virtues and
vices that are mutually exclusive. His characterization of Valentinian naturally follows the same pattern.[2] We can select from
it the good or the bad, to suit our taste. And this method of
judging, recording good and bad by turns, without any attempt
to balance them, is not confined to the character sketch of
which we have spoken—it keeps on appearing on each and
every occasion. There is an injustice in the way in which the
verdict is arrived at and delivered. The attempt to be objective
breaks in the middle.

It has been stated quite recently that, 'although many modi-
fications may be made in detail, it is certain, that Ammianus'
pictures of . . . Valentinian and Valens will stand for ever sub-
stantially unchanged'.[3] But the analysis of the portrait of the
general Ursicinus in Ammianus by E. A. Thompson, who makes
this claim,[4] reflects the same fervent partiality as our investigation of the policy of Valentinian will show, only in the
opposite direction: if Ammianus is guilty of gross exaggerations, if he is reticent on delicate questions which would put
his hero in an unfavourable light, and never suppresses an
irrelevant fact in his effort to paint Ursicinus in the brightest
colours, we shall find the same tricks used to paint Valentinian
and his brother as black as one-sided hatred can contrive. And
Thompson's inquiry into Ammianus' account of the Caesar
Gallus[5] clearly shows the same prejudices: Ammianus conceals
relevant facts, relies maliciously on unwarranted rumours, applies rhetorical artifices and violent phrases to leave a dark

eodem punitus negotio, ea re quod divo Iuliano fuit acceptus, cuius memor-
andis virtutibus ambo fratres principes obtrectabant, nec similes eius nec
suppares'.

[1] E. A. Thompson, op. cit. 13.   [2] xxx. 8 ff.
[3] E. A. Thompson, op. cit. 125.   [4] Ibid. 42 ff.   [5] Ibid. 56 ff.

impression on the minds of his readers of the talented and un-
fortunate Caesar—'a far too gloomy picture'. Finally, that the
policy of Valentinian's right-hand man in Rome, Maximinus,
cannot be condemned as scholars are accustomed with Ammianus to condemn it, that the report of the latter cannot be
taken at its face value, and that Maximinus is depicted by our
great historian as a great deal worse than he was in fact, has
been realized by Thompson too.[1] So it is plain—at least to
me—that this judgement on Valentinian relies on Ammianus
only because he did not undertake the same penetrating
analysis of the real role of our Emperor as of that of the persons mentioned.

It has long been realized how seriously all our authorities are
coloured by the spirit of the age. The Church historians suffer
from sectarian prejudice, their pagan fellows from the abject
flattery and subservience which absolutism brought in its train.
It is quite astonishing to observe how a mouthpiece of senatorial opinion, like Quintus Aurelius Symmachus, could extol
Valentinian to the skies during his lifetime, in a panegyric
delivered in A.D. 370—only to insult him bitterly six years later
when he was dead, and, at the same time, flatter the son who
had succeeded him.[2] Nor is it only the distortion of the literary
genre of the panegyric that is to blame: the orator must share
the guilt. His unreal flatteries must obviously not be taken at
their face value. That means that his serious charges too must
not be accepted without question. But it is not only the wrong
attitude of the ancient writers that has led modern scholars to
an ever-increasing distortion of the picture of Valentinian. A
great modern scholar has his share—perhaps a decisive one—
in the blame. I am thinking of Otto Seeck, who, in a life of
research devoted to the elucidation of countless details of philo-
logy, textual criticism, chronology, prosopography, and numis-
matics, has set the history of the decline of the ancient world
on a new basis. But it is sadly to be regretted that on the
magnificent foundations, laid down in the six volumes of the

---

[1] Ibid. 97 ff., 106.
[2] There is a similar judgement of father and son concerning Valerian and
Gallienus in the Panegyric of Dionysius, Bishop of Alexandria, in Eusebius,
H.E. vii. 10. 2 ff.

Geschichte des Untergangs der antiken Welt, an arbitrary super-structure is often built up by Seeck, leaving the door open to subjective and unstable views; and such is the case here.

On the one hand, Seeck arbitrarily rejects the favourable ver-dict of contemporaries on Valentinian.[1] On the other, he shows equal caprice, when he represents him as a mere German, torn from his original racial environment and completely unable to rise to the height of his calling at the head of a world Empire. Valentinian to him is like a terrible wild beast, breaking out of the primitive forest, to spread nothing but destruction and ruin in the degenerate civilization around him. Just by way of passing comment he observes that he had no brain in his skull[2]—or that he had no taste, because he was amazed by the poetical virtuosity of Ausonius[3]—though the senators shared his amazement. Valentinian could, assuredly, fall into terrible passions, but he was not bloodthirsty.[4] If hostile contempor-aries charge him with envy[5] or reproach him with his arrogance[6] and disastrous greed,[7] we can at least maintain that these faults did not determine the direction of his administration. To repre-sent him as a lazy, painfully cautious man is quite irresponsible and arbitrary. The fact that he was unable, before his elevation, to reach any high rank in the army was due to ill-fortune under Constantius II, to his deliberate and manly conduct under Julian, and not to his being 'destitute of any touch of adventure'.[8] When Ammianus[9] says of him that he was *dux cunctator et tutus*, that does not imply hesitancy or irresolution, but very high praise. That Valens was really lazy *does* follow from our authorities.[10] But that this was due to the conduct of Valen-tinian does not follow from the evidence quoted.[11] If, at the beginning of his reign, he spent half a year on the way from Constantinople to Milan, the reason was not that he chose to travel 'in supreme comfort', but that on his way through the Danube provinces, he held a thorough review of their condition

---

[1] *Gesch. d. Unt. d. ant. Welt*, v. 7.   [2] Ibid. 35, 'sein enges Gehirn'.

[3] Ibid. 41.   [4] Ibid. 41, 'Blutmensch'.

[5] Evidence in ibid. 430 (on p. 17, l. 5).

[6] Ammianus xxvii. 10. 10.   [7] Seeck, op. cit. v. 13.

[8] Ibid. 3.   [9] xxvii. 10. 10.   [10] Cf. Seeck, op. cit. 17.

[11] Ibid. 12.

and investigated the state of the 'limes'. Other charges against him—of evading the hardships of war, of shirking personal command in serious actions, or of choosing to idle the winter away in the warmth of his study, have already been refuted by W. Heering.[1] Nor can I believe that it was mere regard for comfort that made him decline the burden of administering justice in person. In view of the many calls on the Emperor's attention, with wars raging round him, such administration had been no more than an occasional gesture (a survival of the show of constitutional government), never part of a regular programme. Often this 'laziness' is a mere invention.[2] The story of Valentinian sitting at ease in Milan, while the Moors plundered Africa and the Germans Gaul, simply arises from a misunderstanding of the summary sketch of warlike events given by Ammianus at the beginning of the reign of Valentinian, as W. Heering, following N. H. Baynes, has demonstrated. If, on the tidings of the usurpation of Procopius, he did not at once make haste to save his brother, but declared that the war against the Germans was more important, this was no 'feeble waiting on events'.[3] Seeck goes so far as to brand him outright as a coward.[4] He likewise belittles the tremendous efforts of Valentinian to reform the system of frontier defence,[5] as though the idea of the defensive began with him. Actually it came to him as a legacy of centuries; it was the degeneration of the army that compelled him to improve to the utmost the whole technique of defence. Seeck just refuses to recognize the absolute necessity of these exertions and explains them as part of his general inertia. To the same quality he attributes his noble tolerance in religion.[6] But, in this verdict, he finds no modern support.[7]

---

[1] *Kaiser Valentinian der Erste*, Diss. Jena, 1927.

[2] Cf. Seeck, op. cit., v. 14 f., 24 f., 27.   [3] Ibid. 51.

[4] Ibid. 17, based on Ammianus xxx. 8. 11; but, in view of Ammianus xxvii. 10. 10, 11, xxx. 9. 4, and Zosimus iv. 3. 5, he has at least to admit that he possessed enough self-control and steadfastness 'to stand up to his opponent even in the dangers of battle'.

[5] Op. cit. v. 25, 'because any energetic concern was out of keeping with his lazy and negligent mood'.   [6] Ibid. 21.

[7] He is sometimes found contradicting himself, as, for example, ibid. 25, forgetting that he has just expressed himself differently (p. 7, ll. 29 ff.).

Seeck's character-drawing is further deformed by his confusing the qualities of Valentinian with those of his brother, Valens, which here and there resemble his, in many points differ, but are in general weaker. He goes so far as to transfer any unfavourable trait that he finds in Valens to his brother.

But it is inadmissible to weigh the character of Valentinian in the same scales as those of his younger brother. Nor can we accept the assumption of Seeck, that the course of events, at least in the age now in question, was as much determined by the character of the Emperors and their personal decisions as he imagines. The general demoralization at home, the endlessly repeated incursions of foes from abroad, fettered the hands of the Emperor when he made his decisions; for the shaping of his policy the provisions of his predecessors and the earlier course of events were very largely responsible. Even when it was really an individual resolution that marked out the way or decided questions of importance, the Emperor's conduct was still very often determined by the crushing weight of the spirit of the age. It was the high summer of repressions, of prohibitions of the most varied kinds.

The authority of Seeck, backed by his attractive style, has exercised a vast influence[1] and, even if his caricature of Valentinian has not been accepted by all scholars,[2] no one has yet confronted him with a full discovery and description of the part really played by Valentinian. The old way of judging him— more casual, but also more just—has not succeeded in digesting the countless detailed gains of the research of the last decades.[3]

[1] In the sphere of war history W. Heering contradicts him. More justice is done to Valentinian in the short sketch of E. Stein (*Gesch. d. spätrömischen Reiches*, i, 1928, 267), and in the careful summary of A. Nagl (*RE.* vii A, 1948, 2158 ff.). A Solari, *Il rinnovamento dell' impero romano*, 1938, i. 3 ff. has nothing new to add and does not make sufficient use of earlier scholarship (cf. W. Ensslin, *Byz. Zeitschrift*, xli, 1941, 472 ff.).

[2] Cf. E. Korneman in Gercke-Norden, *Einleitung in die Altertumswissenschaft*, iii³, 1933, 121.

[3] Le Nain de Tillemont, *Histoire des empereurs et des princes, etc.*, v, 1732, 1 ff.; E. Gibbon, *Decline and Fall of the Roman Empire*, ed. by J. B. Bury, iii, 1897, 8 ff.; H. Richter, *Das weström. Reich*, 1865, 273; *Cambridge Medieval History*, i, 1927, 218 ff. (N. H. Baynes); H. Schiller, *Gesch. d. röm. Kaiserzeit*, ii, 1887, 352 ff. especially 367 ff. (it is still not out of date).

I cannot undertake to make good this defect here; for the undertaking would take me too far from my own goal. I can only correct the characterization of this hard personality so far as that is necessary to help us to understand his attitude to the Senate.

Valentinian was a native of south Pannonia. His yellow hair, his blue eyes, and his great height are Indo-germanic, bearing in all probability the stamp of the Illyro-Celtic population of that region.[1] We have no reason of any kind to regard him as a German.[2] That part of Pannonia was the most thickly populated and had been least affected by the wars that had raged since the days of Marcus Aurelius, and it included Sirmium, one of the regular imperial residences, as well as Cibalae, the birthplace of Valentinian. His father Gratian by his giant strength and, no doubt, also by his intelligence,[3] had fought his way up from quite a low rank to the position of *comes*, like so many other Pannonian soldiers. One of his grandfathers seems to have borne the name of Valens, like his brother, or else a variant of the name (Valentinus or Valentinianus); but such a name (from a root meaning 'healthy' or 'strong'), is quite in order among Illyrian soldiers.[4]

Before his elevation his career had been undistinguished. In Gaul, where he had commanded a detachment of cavalry under Julian as Caesar, he lost his post through the intrigues of the jealous general, Barbatio, whom Constantius II had sent to supervise the Caesar, his heir.[5] When, under Julian's sole rule, he recovered this position, his deliberate stand as a Christian

[1] On the great stature of the Pannonians cf. Herodian ii. 10. 8.

[2] As does Seeck, op. cit. v. 2 ff. (the evidence is collected, ibid. 421 and 426). He thinks that he was of German blood (ibid. 7). He adapts his characterization to this idea; he derives his loyalty to his friends from the 'German social system' (ibid. 11); he describes his laziness (ibid. 12) and his supposed greed (ibid. 13) as German qualities; again, he emphasizes the 'German morality' that 'was in his blood' (ibid. 20), but then maliciously charges him with 'the savage instincts of his innate barbarism' (ibid. 17, 22). W. Heering follows Seeck (op. cit. 7, 24, 56, 66, 68).

[3] Ammianus xxx. 7. 2: 'ignobili stirpe'; but, according to *Epit. de Caes.* 45. 2, his father came of *mediocri stirpe*, which points to humble, but not barbarian, birth.

[4] See Note 2, p. 128.

[5] For the evidence see the article of A. Nagl, *RE.* vii A. 2159 ff.

forbade any farther advance. Even if he was never banished, as the Church Fathers record, he could not advance in the way that would have been possible if he had trimmed his sails to the breeze of the pagan reaction.[1] This resolute loyalty to conviction must be appraised all the higher because, as appeared later, he was no bigot and, even on the throne, continued to be tolerant of the contrary religious convictions of others. Even so, he became tribune of a distinguished army corps[2] and enjoyed great reputation in the army; for the Emperor Jovian, the successor of Julian, when he fell on the Persian campaign, entrusted him with an important mission and appointed him commander of a detachment of the guard—that is to say, to a post from which he could rise direct to be *magister militum*.[3]

After the sudden death of Jovian on 25 February, A.D. 365, Valentinian came to the throne, in a way unexampled in the annals of Roman imperial elections, with their full tale of low intrigues, brutal murders, bloody rebellions, and civil wars. In itself the case is quite unique. His person was not violently forced on the world, either from above by intrigue or at least at the initiative of court circles, or from below, by riot in the army. No, it was the full and tranquil debate of the highest civilian dignitaries and military leaders of the Empire that declared him the most worthy to wear the purple cloak of the *imperator* and the jewelled diadem.[4] And it had hardly ever yet happened that the new Emperor himself took no part in his own elevation. Valentinian was not in attendance on Jovian, with the mass of the army, on its journey home from the shameful close of the Persian campaign, but was following with his detachment at a distance of several days' march and was quite ignorant of the death of his predecessor or of any intention to

---

[1] O. Seeck, op. cit. v. 3 and 19, and also 422 on p. 3, l. 31, and 431 (p. 19, l. 13). Similarly W. Heering, op. cit. 8 ff.; V. Schultze, *Gesch. d. Untergangs d. gr.-r. Heidentums*, i, 1887, 16; J. Geffcken, *Der Ausgang d. gr.-r. Heidentums*, i, 1920, 293, n. 4; A. Nagl, *RE*. vii A. 2160, &c.

[2] The evidence in A. Nagl, loc. cit.

[3] The evidence in Seeck, op. cit. v. 3 ff., and A. Nagl, loc. cit.

[4] Ammianus xxvi. 1. 3: 'progresso Nicaeam versus exercitu . . . potestatum civilium militiaeque rectores, magnitudine curarum adstricti communium . . . moderatorem quaeritabant, diu exploratum et gravem'.

advance him himself to Empire.[1] The man who recommended Valentinian instead of himself was Saturninius Secundus Salutius,[2] an elderly, cultured dignitary from Gaul—not a Greek, but a distinguished Neoplatonist and champion of Hellenism. He had himself twice received the offer of Empire and was certainly one of the most important figures of the age. Under Julian, Salutius had been civil ruler of the East of the Empire, and although by conviction a philosopher and pagan, he had tried to damp the revolutionary ardour of Julian. Later, under Jovian, he remained *praefectus praetorio*. No better testimonial to Valentinian could be imagined than the recommendation of this independent and high-minded judge. Two considerations may have influenced him in his judgement. One was that the new Emperor was a distinguished and energetic soldier; the storms gathering on all the frontiers forced him to think of that. The other was that he recognized the manifest superiority in strength of Christianity and renounced any violent attempt to impose a pagan régime, but rather sought for the throne a Christian of as moderate a stamp as possible, free from hatred and prejudice, who would not carry on the war of extermination against polytheism. In both directions his choice proved successful. Among the generals in leading positions the Germans, Arinthaeus and Dagalaifus—one an adherent of Julian, the other of Constantius—both supported Valentinian's candidature, as, among the civil dignitaries, did the patrician Datianus, who had himself been proposed as candidate, and others, Christians as well as pagans. The final result was that the leading civil and military authorities of the Empire arrived at a unanimous choice,[3] which was at once ratified by the acclamation of the army.[4] As representative of the higher cul-

---

[1] The evidence is collected, for example, in Seeck, *Gesch. d. Unt. d. ant. Welt.* v. 1 ff. and 421, and A. Nagl, *RE.* vii A. 2161 ff.

[2] Seeck, *RE.* ii A. 2072 ff., who quotes all the sources. Cf. also Seeck, *Die Briefe des Libanius*, 263, 265 ff.; Mommsen, *Hermes*, xxxviii, 1903, 443 ff.; J. R. Palanque, *Essai sur la préfecture de prétoire*, 1933, 38 ff., 44; W. Ensslin, *Mél. Bidez*, 1936, 365 ff.; A. D. Nock, *Sallustius, Concerning the Gods*, 1926, pp. ci ff.; K. F. Stroheker, *Der senatorische Adel im spätantiken Gallien*, 1948, 25 f., 213 ff.; A. Piganiol, *L'Empire chrétien*, 1947, 119, 122, 127, 141, 143, 145, 149 f., 197, 315.

[3] Ammianus xxvi. 1. 5; Socr. *H.E.* 4. 1.   [4] See Note 3, p. 128.

ture, then in ever-growing danger, Salutius was also concerned that the soldier who now donned the purple should be no uneducated clod. It was this concern that caused the suggestion to appoint the distinguished officer, Aequitius, to be rejected.[1]

The proposal of the revered prefect, we must repeat, found unanimous approval; our sources permit no doubt of the absolute unanimity of the choice.[2]

The fact that it was the authority of Salutius that determined the decision did more than thwart the ambitions of certain individuals, ready to fish in troubled waters, more than rule out the influence of the passion and rude violence of the soldier-mob. At the very moment of election it reconciled the one-sided points of view of the two opposing parties. It was not merely the pagan leaders and court cliques of Julian confronting the Christian party of Constantius.[3] The clash between the Western and Eastern army groups also played its part.[4] But there was a third general factor, at least as important as the two just mentioned, which was to fix its stamp on the whole of Valentinian's reign—the rivalry between the various national groups of the Empire, each supplying its representatives to the Court and corps of officers.

[1] Ammianus xxvi. 1. 4 (of the candidates for Empire); 'et rumore tenus, obscuris paucorum susurris, nomen praestringebatur Aequitii, scholae primae Scutariorum etiam tum tribuni, qui cum potiorum auctoritate displicuisset, ut asper et subagrestis, translata est suffragatio levis', &c.

[2] See Note 4, p. 128.

[3] A. Solari, *Klio*, vi, 1933, 332, n. 4.

[4] W. Ensslin, *Byz. Zeitschr.* 1941, 475 ff.; A. Nagl, loc. cit.

THE PANNONIANS AT THE COURT OF VALENTINIAN I

It is a well-known fact that, from A.D. 235 onwards, most of the Emperors came from the Danube and Balkan lands. We also know that it was the Illyrian soldiery which formed the cream of the army and the corps of officers that rose from them and which placed those Emperors on the throne. From Illyricum too came the dynasty of Constantine, though, between Chlorus and Julian, it naturally became more international and lost its local characteristics; its dynastic ideas went beyond its special setting, its marriages blurred the Illyrian picture. Moreover, from Constantine on, the soldiery of the Danube lands was already on the decline. The vast losses of blood, incurred in the uninterrupted wars of so many decades, had undermined its vitality. Yet, in the course of a century, so many Illyrians had found positions at Court, in the imperial guard, and in the officers' corps, that their influence could still on occasion make itself felt, even under the new conditions that followed the extinction of the dynasty of Constantine.

Perhaps it is no accident that already after the death of Julian, a man from those parts came to the throne in the person of Jovian.[1] He was a native of Singidunum (where now the modern Belgrade stands), the son of a popular officer of the guard (*comes domesticorum*). He, like his successor, was an Indo-German, tall and blue-eyed.[2] His father-in-law, Lucillianus,[3] had been *magister militum per Illyricum*, and it is not impossible that he too came of a family from that district. And so it is likely enough that the small group that by a bold stroke forced through the proclamation of Jovian also consisted of his fellow-countrymen.[4]

[1] Evidence in Seeck, *RE*. ix. 2006.
[2] In this district Illyrians, Thracians, and Celts were much intermixed.
[3] Seeck, *RE*. xiii. 1647 ff.
[4] The election of Jovian has been discussed in detail by A. Solari, *Klio*, xxvi, 1933, 330. He is wrong in thinking that the little group which carried

While the high dignitaries had decided at Nicaea on the election of Valentinian and were awaiting his arrival from Ancyra, it was two Pannonians who took the most elaborate precautions to prevent the feelings of the army from veering towards any other candidate. They were out-and-out partisans of their fellow-countryman in his candidature[1] and canvassed for him in the army with all their energy and power.[2] When the superstitious Emperor-to-be arrived and refused to receive the purple on the days that stood under unfavourable signs, it was these same two Pannonians who saw to it that the army should remain quiet and that no serious rival should make his appearance.[3] One of these was Aequitius,[4] commander of the first Guard regiment of the 'Scutarii', then regarded by many as himself worthy of the throne.[5] He was now put at the head of the Illyrian army with the rank of *comes*[6] and, later, on the occasion of the usurpation of Procopius, was promoted to the supreme military rank of *magister militum*.[7] In A.D. 367 he was admitted to the greatest of all Roman distinctions, when he held the ordinary consulship.[8] The second was Leo,[9] then only a subordinate officer under the *magister equitum*, Dagalaifus,[10] but later a *notarius*[11] and finally *magister officiorum* at the side of the new Emperor. He was the bugbear of senatorial society.[12]

---

the election (cf. the words of Ammianus, *tumultuantibus paucis*), 'era costituita di semplici soldati' (op. cit. 331), for *turbine concitato calonum* does not refer to those who set things in motion, but to their blind tools.

[1] Ammianus xxvi. 1. 6: 'ut Pannonii fautoresque principis designati'.

[2] Ibid.: 'exercitus universi iudicium quantum facere nitique poterant . . . firmantes'.   [3] Ibid. 2. 1.

[4] Seeck, *RE*. vi. 321 ff.; C. Patsch, *Beiträge zur Völkerkunde von Südosteuropa*, iv, 1929, 33 (Sitz.-Ber. Wiener Akad., Band ccix, 5. Abh.); E. A. Thompson, op. cit. 98 f.   [5] Ammianus xxvi. 1. 4 and 6.

[6] Ibid. 5. 3.

[7] Ibid. 5. 11; cf. A. Nagl, *RE*. vii A. 2105, 2170.

[8] Ammianus xxx. 3. 1 and the *fasti consulares*.

[9] For his career cf. A. E. R. Boak–J. E. Dunlap, *Two Studies in Later Roman and Byzantine Administration* (Univ. of Michigan Stud., Human. Ser. xiv), 1924, 106 f.

[10] Ammianus xxvi. 1. 6: 'adhuc sub Dagalaifo magistro equitum rationes numerorum militarium tractans'.   [11] Ibid. xxviii. 1. 12 ff.

[12] Ibid.: 'exitialis postea magister officiorum'. Cf. E. A. Thompson, op. cit. 103, 105.

It can be understood, then, that, when Valentinian began to reign and, a month later, appointed his younger brother, Valens, his colleague, their Pannonian friends and relatives crowded into the court offices and high army commands. We must not forget that the high officials at that time were seldom retained in office for more than one or two years, and so replacement was a far simpler matter than it is today. There was the further point that Julian only recently had dismissed the Christian dignitaries of Constantius[1] and that Valentinian and Valens now withdrew the administration of the provinces and other important civil and military posts, with few exceptions, from Julian's nominees.[2] Thus it was that a whole series of key positions changed hands.

Now, too, began the upward trend in the career of a Pannonian of great talent, who ruled with a firm hand and who was described in senatorial circles as the evil genius of Valentinian[3] —Maximinus. His grandfather came from the free Dacian tribe of the Carpi, whom Diocletian had settled in the south-east of Pannonia. His father was keeper of records to the civil governor of the province, but he took care that his son should receive a good education, which enabled him to begin his career as an advocate and then become, in turn, governor of Corsica, Sardinia, and Etruria,[4] and *praefectus annonae* in the old capital. After having received criminal jurisdiction in the ugly cases of high treason and like offences—we shall return to this matter later—he became *vicarius* of Rome and, finally, *praefectus praetorio Galliarum*[5]—only to crash the more disastrously, when, on the death of Valentinian, the senatorial reaction gained the upper hand. His son, Marcellianus, obtained a military command in his native land of Valeria, i.e. the eastern border of

[1] Socrat. *H.E.* iii. 13; Sozom. *H.E.* v. 18. Cf., for example, V. Schulze, *Gesch. d. Untergangs. d. gr.-r. Heidentums*, i, 1887, 144 ff.; J. Geffcken, *Kaiser Iulianus*, 1914, 110; J. Bidez, *La Vie de l'empereur Julien*, 1930, 263 ff.

[2] Zosimus iv. 2. 3. Salutius was not dismissed at the time, as Zosimus reports, but somewhat later. [3] Ammianus xxix. 3. 1 and 2.

[4] Ibid. xxviii. I. 5-7. Other evidence is collected by W. Ensslin in *RE.* Suppl. v. 663 f., no. 5; A. Nagl, op. cit. 2191 f.; O. Seeck, *Regesten der Kaiser u. Päpste.* 1919, 32, 131, 147.

[5] J. R. Palanque, *Essai sur la préfecture du prétoire. . .* , 1933, 40 ff. Cf. W. Ensslin, *Byz. Zeitschr.* xxxvi, 1936, 325 on his vicariate.

Pannonia, at quite an early age, as was then customary.[1] The brother of his wife, Valentinus, who for a serious offence had been banished to Britain, instigated a revolt there.[2]

To the same society belonged the first *magister officiorum* of the new Emperor, the Dalmatian Ursacius, who is described by Ammianus, not without suspicion of prejudice, as a rough, furious, and savage man.[3] There was also Viventius of Siscia, who together with Ursacius served Valentinian as *quaestor sacri palatii*,[4] and, later, became governor of Rome[5] and then *praefectus praetorio Galliarum*.[6] The senatorial circles, so bitter in their hatred of their Pannonian rivals, made an exception of Viventius; they praise his blamelessness in office and his keen intelligence.[7] In Gaul, too, his administration was excellent. We know that he made a clearance of many subordinate officers who were harming the commonweal.[8]

The Pannonian Leo, who at the time of Valentinian's accession was on the staff of the *magister equitum* as a sort of adjutant,[9] later became imperial *notarius* and, in this capacity, shared with Maximinus the conduct of the *causes célèbres* in Rome[10] and was then *magister officiorum* at court.[11] His activities had drawn on to him the hatred of the senatorial circles.[12]

One is struck at once by the number of Pannonian officials who received posts of high confidence in Rome. It was no accident that the important post of *vicarius urbis* was held, after Maximinus and Ursacius, by another man from the same circle, Simplicius of Emona, the intimate friend of Maximinus, who began as a *grammaticus*, then as *consiliarius* came into the

[1] A. Alföldi, *Budapest Története*, i, 1943, 684 ff.; E. A. Thompson, op. cit. 98 f., 100.

[2] Ammianus xxviii. 3. 3–6; O. Seeck, *Hermes*, xli, 1906, 322; A. Nagl, *RE*. vii A. 2175; W. Ensslin, *RE*. vii A. 2274, no. 7.

[3] Ammianus xxvi. 4. 4 and 5. 7.　　　　　　　　　　[4] Ibid. 4. 4.

[5] Ibid. xxvii. 3. 11.　　　　　　　　　　[6] J. R. Palanque, op. cit. 40.

[7] Ammianus, loc. cit.: 'integer et prudens Pannonius'.

[8] *Cod. Theod.* xii. 12. 3, 4, 6; cf. Seeck, *Gesch. d. Unt. d. ant. Welt*, v. 14.

[9] Ammianus xxvi. 1. 6: 'adhuc sub Dagalaifo magistro equitum rationes numerorum militarium tractans'.

[10] Ibid. xxviii. 1. 12.

[11] Ibid. xxx. 2. 10 and 5. 10, cf. xxviii. 1. 41.

[12] Cf. p. 14, n. 12 and p. 69, n. 6.

entourage of his patron, and after being provincial governor and *consularis* of Numidia reached the office of *vicarius*.[1]

We hear of another Illyrian, Diocles, that he was chief finance minister (*comes sacrarum largitionum*),[2] and that the brother of his wife, Constantianus, held the post of chief groom (*tribunus stabuli*) beside Valentinian,[3] whilst his elder brother, Cerealis also reached the same high rank.[4] These are pieces of information that have chanced to come down to us; actually such cases must have been much more numerous.

If men from Pannonia and the neighbouring lands swarmed round Valentinian, such friends and relatives seem to have been present in even greater numbers in the entourage of Valens.[5]

In the first place, we find beside him his father-in-law, Petronius, who as commander of a detachment of infantry reached at one leap the supreme rank of *patricius*, and who, while screwing up the collection of taxes to a terrifying intensity, himself, to the detriment of others, attained great wealth, and thus very soon earned the hatred of all.[6] He built up a regular clique (*factio*) round himself, and it was probably he who was responsible for the dismissal of the old *praefectus praetorio*, Salutius, in order to be able to put his own confidant, Nebridius, in his place.[7] Another Pannonian and old crony of Valens was Serenianus,[8] the commander of the most distinguished troop of the guard (*schola domesticorum*), described in the senatorial tradition as an uneducated clown.[9] One more courtier of the same origin, a relative of Valens, was that Aequitius who held the post of *cura palatii* when he and his master both fell victims to the disaster of Adrianople.[10]

---

[1] Ammianus xxviii. 1. 45 ff.; Seeck, *RE*. iii A. 203.

[2] Ammianus xxvii. 7. 5; Seeck, *RE*. v. 796, no. 44.

[3] Ammianus xxviii. 2. 10.   [4] Ibid. xxx. 5. 19, 10. 4.

[5] How deeply Valens loved his countrymen, in the narrower sense, is revealed in a passage of Ammianus (xxvi. 10. 1): 'incultis moribus homo . . . Valenti . . . ob similitudinem morum et genitalis patriae vicinitatem acceptus'.

[6] Ibid. 7 ff., 17.

[7] Ibid. 7. 4; Seeck, *Gesch. d. Unt. d. ant. Welt*, v. 20 and 46; A. Nagl, *RE*. vii A. 2099; W. Ensslin, *Mélanges Bidez*, 1934, 372 ff.

[8] Ammianus xxvi. 5. 3: 'ut Pannonius sociatusque Valenti'.

[9] Ibid. 5. 3, 10. 1–2. But cf. E. A. Thompson, op. cit. 63.

[10] Ammianus xxxi. 12. 15, 13, 18.

These friends and kinsmen of Valens caused him many difficulties by their selfishness; here, we may well believe the unfriendly tradition. To them was attributed the fact that Valens, though in general competent, entrusted the administration of justice to his officials and did not concern himself with it in person, as Julian had done, thus allowing the cancer of the age to grow unchecked. The military commanders and courtiers were able, without hindrance, to bribe the judges and advocates, to the immense loss of the small man.[1]

But it is a mistake to suppose[2] that this Pannonian society was any worse than the rest. It is, after all, a typical symptom of this decadent age that cliques should flourish on every side. In A.D. 367, for example, when Valentinian fell seriously ill in Rheims and it was feared that he might die, the Gauls who happened to be about him put their heads together[3] to discuss whom they should make his successor. Again, when, after the death of Valentinian, Ausonius, the tutor of his son, snatched the reins of government in the West, he secured his own appointment, first as chief of the Western administration (*praefectus praetorio Galliarum*) and, in A.D. 379, as ordinary consul. Over and above all this he got his son, Hesperius, appointed first *proconsul Africae*, then immediately afterwards *praefectus praetorio* of the Italian diocese at the court of the still boyish Valentinian II. But even that was not enough. He caused his old father, a simple Gallic doctor, to be distinguished with the title of a *praefectus praetorio Illyrici*, and his son-in-law, Thalassius, to be raised to be *vicarius* of Macedonia and, later, *proconsul Africae*. The son of his sister, Arborius, became, in A.D. 379, chief finance minister (*comes sacrarum largitionum*) and, after that, governor of Rome (*praefectus urbi*). The sons-in-law of his sister and even the husband of his granddaughter all obtained fat jobs. And Ausonius is not in the least ashamed of his horrible greediness, but boasts of it to the world in his

---

[1] Ammianus xxx. 4. 1 ff.

[2] As did C. Patsch, *Beiträge zur Völkerkunde von Südosteuropa*, iv, 1929, 33 ff.

[3] Ammianus xxvii. 6. 1: 'conloquio occultiore Gallorum, qui aderant in commilitio principis'. Cf. on the *factio* of the Gauls at Court K. F. Stroheker, *Der senatorische Adel im spätantiken Gallien*, 1948, 26 f.

poems.[1] But wherever we can lift the veil however slightly, we find the same abuses everywhere. For example, when Tatianus under Theodosius became *praefectus praetorio Orientis*, we find his son *praefectus urbi* in Constantinople and, doubtless, a whole crowd of these folk pushed into office in their train. Theodosius, too, showed no less favour to his Spanish countrymen than Valentinian had shown to his Pannonian adherents.[2] We can assert without fear of contradiction that whenever anyone in the fourth century secured an office, he at once brought in his dependants and friends with him.[3] In particular, we must be careful not to suppose that the most cultured, wealthy, and ancient Roman classes acted any differently in the matter. When we read through the letters of recommendation that Symmachus wrote by the hundred, we see at a glance how those threads were spun in which one clique or the other could entangle the whole Empire, in order to suck its blood, like a spider in its corner. Ammianus, who, for all his sympathy with the aristocracy of Rome, had a strong sense of decency, expresses himself in very plain terms about the head of a great *gens*. 'Like a fish gasping out its life out of water, he suffered torments if he failed to secure one of the governorships (*praefecturae praetorio*) of one of the great sections of the Empire. And the great families, abusing their position, were always goading him on to this end. Unbounded greed was their sin from of old, and they would force the head of the house into public life, in order thereby to assure themselves of greater gains without fear of punishment.'[4]

[1] For all details see O. Seeck, *Gesch. d. Unt. d. ant. Welt*, v. 41 ff., and K. F. Stroheker, op. cit. 150, no. 51, with lit.; Ch. Favez, *Museum Helveticum*, 1946, 11 ff.

[2] *Epit. de Caes.* 48. 9, 18. The most remarkable is the splendid career of Cynegius, whose rise began with the proclamation of his countryman Theodosius. Cf. Seeck, *RE*. xi. 252 f.

[3] Cf. O. Seeck in his edition of Symmachus (*Mon. Germ. Hist., auct. ant.* vi. 1, 1882), p. xlvi.

[4] Ammianus xxvii. 11. 3 (on Petronius Probus, the mighty head of the family of the Christian Anicii): 'atque ut natantium genus, elemento suo expulsum, haut ita diu spirat in terris, ita ille marcebat absque praefecturis, quas iugi familiarum licentia capere cogebatur, numquam innocentium per cupiditates immensas, utque multa perpetrarent impune, dominum suum mergentium in rem publicam'.

But we must not look at this system of family cliques with our modern eyes. That a mass of protégés should gather round Roman notables of influence was not a symptom of the age of decay; it had been a main feature of the healthy old Roman development,[1] as, too, was the extension of a net of interests round the great families.[2]

However, in the later Roman period, the demands on liberality to kinsmen, friends, and clients,[3] far from diminishing, tended to increase.[4] In the eyes of Eutropius, whose distinguished career ran under and after Valens, to enrich and exalt your friends was a moral obligation,[5] and he records statistically of the Emperors how they met it. Even the Emperors themselves felt this obligation—the puritanical Julian[6] no less than his spendthrift predecessors. People even went so far as to maintain that the public funds were better placed in private pockets than under official lock and key.[7] This passion to endow and enrich others, these *profusiones immodicae*, grew to be a madness, and, even if 'it was Constantine who was the first of all (Emperors) to open the throttles of his friends, it was Constantius who fed them with the flesh and blood of the provinces'.[8]

In contrast to this, the economy of Valentinian, even if interpreted as greed, represented a healthy reaction; so, too, did his conduct in excluding his kinsmen from high positions and large revenues in far greater measure than either his predecessors or

[1] See the apposite comments of L. Wickert, *Klio*, xxxiv, 1941, 151 ff.

[2] Cf. F. Muenzer, *Adelsparteien und Adelsfamilien*, 1920; R. Syme, *The Roman Revolution*, 1939; H. H. Scullard, *Roman Politics*, Oxford, 1951.

[3] Characteristic, e.g. Cassius Dio xliv. 39. 1 ff. (on Caesar).

[4] Cf. A. Alföldi, *Die Kontorniaten*, 1942-3, 40 ff.

[5] Eutropius, *Brev.* 10. 7, 2 (on Constantine): 'adfectatur iusti amoris, quem omni sibi et liberalitate et docilitate quaesivit, sicut in nonnullos amicos dubius, ita in reliquos egregius, nihil occasionum praetermittens, quo opulentiores eos clarioresque praestaret'.

[6] Ibid. 10. 15: 'familiarium etiam locupletator neque inhonores sinens, quorum laboriosa expertus fuisset officia'. 16: 'in amicos liberalis, sed minus diligens, quam tantum principem decuit. fuerunt enim nonnulli, qui vulnera gloriae eius inferrent'. [7] See Note 5, p. 129.

[8] Ammianus xvi. 8. 12: 'proximorum fauces aperuit primus omnium Constantinus, sed eos medullis provinciarum saginavit Constantius'. Cf. also Seeck, *Gesch. d. Unt. d. ant. Welt*, iv. 394 (on l. 21 of p. 33).

his successors.[1] He also took extraordinary pains in choosing his high officials.[2]

On the contrary, it is true that, with his deep love for his home in the narrower sense,[3] he, like his brother, was very dependent on his old friends.[4] 'But this ready reliance on the honour of his friends often passed over into a careless and excessive trustfulness, such as the corrupt officials of the age nowise merited. . . ., If the Emperors had once appointed a man to office, they regarded him as one on whom they could unreservedly rely. They retained him all the longer in office and were deaf to the complaints of the oppressed. Valentinian went so far that, if anyone appealed to him to reject a judge in a case as a personal enemy, he would refer the matter to that very judge. He even objected to settling appeals himself. If ever a party to a case ventured to come to court to further his cause by personal intercession, he fined him a sum amounting to half the amount under dispute. Even when deputations from cities submitted complaints, he was disinclined to give a personal decision; they had to submit their petition to the *praefectus praetorio*, who could decide the matter at his pleasure, whether or no the affair deserved the attention of the supreme authority. This meant, of course, that the subjects were delivered up unprotected to the caprice of the officials. It was uncommonly hard to convince the Emperors that their creatures could be thieves and oppressors: they reposed an absolute confidence in them and were completely satisfied if the taxes flowed in punctually.'[5]

[1] Ammianus xxx. 9. 2: '. . . petulantiam frenarat aulae regalis, quod custodire facile potuit, necessitudinibus suis nihil indulgens, quas aut in otio reprimebat aut mediocriter honoravit, absque fratre, quem temporis compulsus angustiis in amplitudinis suae societatem adsumpsit'.

[2] Ibid. 9. 3: 'scrupulosus in deferendis potestatibus celsis', &c.; also of Valens (xxxi. 14. 2): 'pervigil semper et anxius, ne quis propinquitatem eius praetendens, altius semet efferret'.

[3] Hieron. *ep.* 60. 15. 3, on his death: 'Valentinianus vastato genitali solo et inultam patriam derelinquens vomitu sanguinis extinctus est'.

[4] Ammianus xxx. 9. 2, xxxi. 14. 2; *Epit. de Caes.* 45. 6 and 46. 3, &c.

[5] Seeck, *Gesch. d. Unt. d. ant. Welt*, v. 11–13, with the evidence of the sources. Cf. also J. R. Palanque, op. cit. 37 ff., 47; E. Stein, op. cit. i. 267 and 275.

Besides the Pannonians, Dalmatians, and Moesians, we do, of course, find the sons of other provinces at the court of the two imperial brothers and in their bureaux. Remigius, for example, the *magister officiorum*, who concealed and hushed up from Valentinian the scandalous abuses of his kinsman, Romanus, the notorious *comes Africae*, came from Mainz.[1] Doryphorianus, the *vicarius urbis Romae* about A.D. 374, one of the intimates of Maximinus, was a Gaul;[2] besides him, there were, of course, many other Gauls at court,[3] as we have seen. From Mauretania came Eupraxius,[4] the independent confidant of Valentinian, who gallantly supported his opinion even against the Emperor in a case that he felt to be just. He was first *magister memoriae*, then, after A.D. 367, *quaestor sacri palatii* at least till 371, then in 374 governor of Rome. From Antioch came the cultured Ampelius, the *magister officiorum*, then, after his *gemini proconsulatus*, *praefectus urbi*.[5] In the army, a great part was played by the German generals, such as Charietto,[6] or the *magister militum*, Dagalaifus, who was an ordinary consul in the year A.D. 366,[7] or Nevitta, who had already held the ordinary consulship under Julian,[8] and others. Among the Germans, too, we find many a *comes*, *dux*, and *tribunus*, as their names, Nannienus, Fullofaudes, Frigeridus, Charietto, Balchobaudes, Fraomarus, Bitheridus, Hortarius, Mallobaudes, and the rest prove. Among the generals of Valens we find, besides Germans such as Vadomarius, the king of the Alamanni, Arintheus, the *magister militum*, and also an officer of Iazygian-Sarmatian birth, the *magister equitum* Victor.[9]

[1] Seeck, *RE*. i A. 594; K. F. Stroheker, op. cit. 207, no. 321.

[2] Seeck, *RE*. v. 1579; K. F. Stroheker, op. cit. 164, no. 107.

[3] Ammianus xxvii. 6. 1; K. F. Stroheker, op. cit. 26 f.

[4] Seeck, *RE*. vi. 1237; E. A. Thompson, op. cit. 16, 20, 139.

[5] Ammianus xxviii. 4. 3; Seeck, *RE*. i. 1881 and *Gesch. d. Unt. d. ant. Welt*, v. 404; E. Groag, *Die Reichsbeamten von Achaia in spätrömischer Zeit* (Diss. Pann. ser. i. 14), 1946, 38, 40 ff., 76, 82.

[6] Seeck, *RE*. iii. 2139; A. Piganiol, *L'Empire chrétien*, 1947, 121, 125, 174, 262.

[7] Seeck, *RE*. iv. 1983 ff.; A. Piganiol, op. cit. 125, 142, 145, 149 f., 153, 174, 184.

[8] Ensslin, *RE*. xvii. 156 ff.; A. Piganiol, op. cit. 125 ff., 142, 145.

[9] Ammianus xxxi. 12. 6; A. Piganiol, op. cit. 142, 145, 153, 156, 158, 184, 206.

It has already been observed that among all these men of the most varied nationalities it is only quite rarely that a scion of the old senatorial families appears; but that does not mean that they were completely absent. In the list of provincial governors a number of senators of lower rank could be enumerated. But it will be enough to observe that, even under Valentinian, Aginatius, a member of the great house of the Anicii, was *vicarius Romae*[1] and that Vulcacius Rufinus, a scion of one of the greatest of the aristocratic families, was, until his death, *praefectus praetorio Italiae* at the side of Valentinian.[2] His successor, Petronius Probus, was the head of the ancient house of the Anicii, just mentioned, with their prodigious wealth.

There are passages in Ammianus' history which show that Probus[3] was no better than any of his contemporaries among the Emperor's leading men. And yet the Empire might have expected something better from him; 'throughout the Roman world, over which his possessions were scattered, he was everywhere famous for his brilliant descent, his power, and his wealth', so writes Ammianus,[4] 'but whether he had won his wealth honestly is not for a modest writer like me to say'. He falls under the condemnation that we mentioned above. The great aristocratic families forced the heads of their houses on the State, in order to cover up their criminal tricks and satisfy their boundless lust for gold.[5] Of all these swollen oligarchs Probus was in his time the most powerful.[6] Beginning in A.D. 367, in his thirty-third year, he went on, changing but never stopping for practically two decades, as governor of the dioceses of Italy, Illyricum, North Africa, and Gaul. A single detail is characteristic of him: when he had in 376 for a short time to leave the first of the prefectures mentioned, he simply played it into the hands of his father-in-law.[7]

---

[1] Ammianus xxviii. 1. 32; Seeck, *RE.* i. 809 ff.

[2] Ammianus xxviii. 11. 1; Seeck, *Gesch. d. Unt. d. ant. Welt*, v. 426 (on l. 32 of p. 11).

[3] The evidence about this man is collected in Seeck, *RE.* i. 2205 ff.

[4] Ammianus xxvii. 11. 1.

[5] Ibid. 11. 3.

[6] Ibid. xxviii. 1. 31: 'Probi ... viri summatum omnium maximi'.

[7] The information about the prefectures of Probus is imperfect and gives rise to some thorny questions which cannot be answered with certainty; cf.

No more attractive is the character-sketch given of Probus by our historian, despite all the reticence inspired by his sympathies for Rome. When the Iazyges and Quadi, harrying Pannonia, were swarming round Sirmium, Probus fell into such a panic, unused as he was to war's alarms, that he had express teams ready, and, had he not feared that the whole city would follow him, he would have left everyone in the lurch to save his own skin.[1] When he comes up against a man of resolution he gives way; but if anyone approaches him timidly, he plays the part of the man of steel.[2] He is suspicious, and that makes him often hurt when he seems to favour a person; if he once takes it into his head to get rid of anyone, he is absolutely merciless.[3] He is a deadly intriguer,[4] and mischief can come of his bloodthirsty quarrelsomeness.[4] When the Pannonian, Maximinus, was *praefectus annonae* in Rome and ventured to interfere in Probus' sphere of interests, Probus was afraid to join issue with the confidant of the Emperor; he secretly passed over to Maximinus a letter sent him by another Anicius, bringing charges against Maximinus, and thereby effected the ruin of that kinsman who trusted him.[5]

To his friends and adherents he is generous,[6] doubtless in order to insure his own position thereby. Even if he never commands his clients and servants to break the law, he nevertheless defends them at all costs, whatever their offence, without respect for right, for God or man.[7] He exploits his high position to enrich himself.[8] In order to prolong his enjoyment of office he discards his aristocratic pride and flatters his master with a complete lack of shame.[9] Valentinian lent him his complete confidence and not only gave him the ordinary consulship, usually reserved for members of the dynasty and the most important *viri militares*, but let him share the honour with the

---

Seeck, *RE.* i. 2206; E. Stein, *Rhein. Mus.* lxxiv, 1925, 364 ff., 377 ff.; J. R. Palanque, op. cit. 109 ff.

[1] Ammianus xxix. 6. 9 f.

[2] Ibid. xxvii. 11. 2–3.

[3] Ibid. 11. 5–6.

[4] Ibid. 2.

[5] Ibid. xxviii. 1. 31–3.

[6] Ibid. xxvii. 11. 2.

[7] Ibid. 4.

[8] Ibid. 1, &c.; Seeck, *RE.* i. 2206.

[9] Ammianus xxx. 5. 4: 'non ut prosapiae suae claritudo monebat, plus adulationi quam verecundiae dedit'.

young Augustus, Gratian, the highest distinction possible.[1] Let us listen to Ammianus recounting, in his florid and bombastic style, the crooked ways that Probus followed in trying brutally to oppress the subjects and secure the favour of the sovereign, till finally, shortly before his death, Valentinian stumbled on his intrigues:[2]

'Valentinian directed his exasperation and fury entirely on Probus, never, from the moment that he had seen through him, ceasing to threaten or relenting. For everyone knew the cause and, indeed, it was not obscure and no slight one. Probus had not only just then obtained the position of *praefectus praetorio*, but had also been trying, in any and every conceivable way, to extend his tenure of it. Nor did he rely, as his descent and reputation should have required of him, on decency and modesty, but on abject flattery. When he realized the spirit of his Emperor, who grasped at any way of making money . . . he followed him to any lengths. The subject population suffered heavily. The fatal justifications that he found for his taxes ruined the already crumbling prosperity of rich and poor alike. Pretext followed pretext, each time worse, as that ancient method of bloodletting easily suggested to him. The steady growth of the pressure of taxation and other charges finally drove even the nobles, in fear of the worst, to desert their homes. Others, already squeezed out by the terrible oppressions of the tax-collectors and left with no means of payment, became permanent occupants of the prisons. Some of them, weary of life in such a world, were glad to cure their ills by hanging themselves. Rumours got abroad that violence and inhumanity were steadily on the increase, but Valentinian took as little notice, as if his ears had been stopped with wax. . . . Revenue was all that he thought of; and yet he might have had mercy on Pannonia, his own home, sooner, if he had known how pitilessly it was being exploited. It was too late when he became enlightened; it happened through the accident that I shall describe. The *praefectus praetorio* compelled Epirus, with the rest of his provinces, to record its official thanks to him. (We actually possess inscriptional evidence of cities and provinces recording the supposed benefits of Probus by erecting statues or sending embassies.[3]) Epirus, therefore, dispatched an embassy and compelled a philosopher, named Iphicles, a man of unusual strength of mind, to discharge the task. When he set eyes on the Emperor and when the Emperor recognized him and asked him why

[1] As Seeck has already emphasized, *RE*. i. 2206.
[2] Ammianus xxx. 5. 4 ff.
[3] The evidence is collected in Seeck, *RE*. i. 2206.

he had come, Iphicles answered him in Greek. When the Emperor pressed him to tell him whether those who had sent him, at the bottom of their hearts, thought well of the prefect, he, like a true philosopher and champion of truth, replied that their thanks came "reluctantly and with groans". This reply struck the Emperor like a spear-thrust through the heart. Like a bloodhound on the trail, he began to track down Probus. In confidential talks with provincials whom he knew, he asked where this man and that was, naming men distinguished by honourable position or family, where such-and-such a rich man or leading member of the city-council was to be found. But, when he learned that one had been hanged, . . . another had committed suicide, a third had died under the scourge (at the criminal examination), he broke out into an alarming passion. The gathering fire of his anger kindled Leo also, who was then *magister officiorum* and, shameful to say, wanted to become prefect himself—only to fall the deeper thereafter. Had he reached that position, he would have done such things as must have made men extol the administration of Probus in comparison with them. . . .'

Ammianus, certainly following a senatorial source, makes Valentinian himself partly to blame for the ill deeds of Probus. Valentinian, he says, cared nothing for justice when money had to be procured,[1] and took offence at nothing that might bring in even the least profit.[2] He repeats the same charges later, but adds that the excuse was usually given that the State chest had been emptied by the defeat at the hands of the Persians and that Valentinian, in thus intensifying his cruelty and his greed, was really concerned to procure war material and expenses for his army. He goes on to show, by classical examples, that he ought not to have done so.[3]

But all his comparisons are, of course, very lame. What is certain is that Valentinian was reviled in Rome as avaricious and cruel,[4] but there was malice in the charges. Jerome, the

---

[1] Ammianus xxx. 5. 5 (on Probus): 'contemplatus enim propositum principis, quaerendae undique pecuniae vias absque iustorum iniustorumque discretione scrutantis, errantem non reducebat ad aequitatis tramitem (ut saepe moderatores fecere tranquilli) sed ipse quoque flexibilem sequebatur atque traversum. unde graves oboedientium casus', &c.

[2] Ibid. 7: 'Valentinianus viro tamquam auribus cera inlitis ignorabat, indifferenter quidem lucrandi vel ex rebus minimis avidus, idque tantum cogitans, quod offerebatur'.   [3] See Note 6, p. 129.

[4] See Note 7, p. 129.

great Father of the Church from Pannonia or Dalmatia, who was living in Rome at the time, is certainly more correct in his judgement when he says: 'But Valentinian was an excellent Emperor, like Aurelian in his ways, except that some explained his excessive severity as cruelty and his economy as greed.'[1] That this was really the case is proved by our own witness for the Crown, Ammianus, who, at another point, when he is not tied by his source, declares: 'To the inhabitants of the provinces he was indulgent, everywhere mitigating the burden of taxation.'[2]

Moreover, we know that Valentinian, though he allowed the taxes to be collected brutally, was considerate enough to reduce them whenever it was at all possible, that he economized, put the brake on merciless collectors, abolished such exemptions from taxation as had been secured by favour, and punished with extreme severity the abuses of the tax-officials.[3] Thus he held the reins of administration firmly in his hands. We may, therefore, again credit Jerome,[4] who, writing immediately after the events, says: 'Probus, the prefect of Illyricum, by excessive injustice in the collection of taxes ruined the provinces, committed to his charge, even before the barbarians (the Goths, Alans, and Huns) had devastated them.' It was Probus, then, who was guilty, and this comes out clearly when we read with attention the passage of Ammianus, quoted above, in which he records the activities of the too powerful prefect.

---

[1] Hieron. *Chron.* A.D. 365 (p. 224. 8, Helm): 'Valentinianus egregius alias imperator et Aureliani similis, nisi quod severitatem eius nimiam et parcitatem quidam crudelitatem et avaritiam interpretabantur'. Cf. also *Chron. Pasch.* 557 (Bonn) = *Chron. min.* ed. Mommsen, i (*Mon. Germ. Hist., auct. ant.* ix), p. 241, ad a. 369.

[2] Ammianus xxx. 9. 1 (on Valentinian): 'in provinciales admodum parcus, tributorum ubique molliens sarcinas'.

[3] The details are given by Seeck, *Gesch. d. Unt. d. ant. Welt*, v. 13; W. Heering, *Kaiser Valentinianus*, i, 1927, 59; A. Nagl, *RE*. vii A. 2188 ff.

[4] Hieron. *Chron.* A.D. 371 (p. 246. 18, Helm). Cf. Mommsen, *Ges. Schr.* vii. 604; Seeck, *RE*. i. 2206; R. Egger, *Byzantion*, v, 1929–30, 19.

III

CORRUPTION AND ITS ANTIDOTE, TERRORISM

THE decay of the life of late Rome, and the brutality with which men tried to arrest the decline, had begun long before the reign of Valentinian, and they were to become even worse after him. Before we pass on to describe the frictions between Emperor and Senate, we must first cast a glance at these evils in order to be able to judge those frictions in a wider context and from a higher point of view.

One symptom, characteristic of the break-up of the late Roman world, was the corruption that poisoned the whole body politic. Otto Seeck, in his great work devoted to the decline of the ancient world, has drawn a grim and faithful picture of it. It would be no hard task to throw new light on it from other sides and to enliven the pictures with new colours. The material is always to hand in plenty. But we prefer, out of respect for the classical performance of Seeck, to select from his account those essential features which are all that the reader, who is not a professional researcher, needs in order to realize the extent of that evil, adding a few extra notes of our own.[1]

The terrible convulsions of the third century after Christ had ruined the material resources of the Empire, annihilated its spiritual energy and its moral reserves, and had accelerated, in an alarming degree, the decline that had already set in before. Diocletian and his successors had had to use violent measures to bring some kind of order back to this state of demoralization. They crushed society in the iron clamp of castes, separated from one another by barriers that could not be passed. By breaking up the great administrative districts and enormously multiplying the army of officials, they secured an ever severer control of their subjects. The yield of taxation, too, which had seriously declined through the general impoverishment, the decay of agriculture and business, could only be raised by

[1] For the details see Seeck, *Gesch. d. Unt. d. ant. Welt*, ii², 1921, 101 ff. and 330 ff., with modern literature and quotations from the ancient authorities.

brutal oppression, just high enough to allow the cumbrous machinery of government to continue working.

The squeeze of the tax-press and the inhumanity in collection that went with it had been getting worse since the third century.[1] But, parallel with them, grew those crafty turns and twists by which men tried to escape from the caste system and the burden of taxes. For example we know in detail just how the members of the city councils, the *decuriones*, aimed at escaping from the burdens of their now hereditary rank—using those very prescriptions by which the imperial edicts had tried to make such evasion impossible.[2] This once prosperous and self-assured middle class was now threatened, in case of failure to deliver the taxes, not only with the confiscation of its property, but with the torture, the knout, and the prison, and even with the death penalty itself.[3]

Anyone, then,

'who possessed money and influence and was clever and energetic, no longer used his capabilities and possibilities, as in the good old days, for the benefit of his city, but only to free himself of his fetters. Nor was such endeavour as hopeless as the severity of the laws seems to imply. If the man in question could once win over a skilful courtier, able to take advantage of the Emperor in a moment of weakness, he might easily succeed in being taken into one of the imperial offices, or even, if he was wealthy enough, in getting into the Senate of Rome or Constantinople. . . . If you could not get near the Emperor, you might contrive by bribery or flattery to get an officer to insert your name in his corps or a governor to smuggle you into his bureau. Exemptions from the local senates, therefore, became ever more frequent, and complaints kept reaching the court that the senates were shrivelling up and failing to discharge their financial obligations. The Emperor would then issue a new law, thundering out his wrath and declaring all exceptional exemptions as null and void and cancelling the validity of his concessions. That meant that you had to return to your hated *ordo*, and the heavy price that you had paid in bribery was lost. But, if you were clever enough to find a good hiding-place, you might still escape the danger

[1] For the details, see Seeck, op. cit. ii². 270 ff.; U. Brasiello, *La repressione penale nel diritto romano*, 1937, 450 ff.; R. Monier, *Manuel élémentaire de droit romain*, i⁶, 1947, 190 ff.; E. Levy, *Gesetz und Richter im kais. Strafrecht*, i (Bull. dell' Inst. d. diritto rom. xlv, 1938); A. Ehrhardt *RE*, 6a. 1775 f.

[2] *Cod. Theod.* xiii. 1 ff.   [3] For the details see Seeck, op. cit. 330 ff.

that threatened you, and your example would encourage your companions in misery to try the same trick. Many sought refuge in the bosom of the Church, by becoming priests or monks. This method helped for a time, but only gave rise to a fresh hunt for decurions. Others married the slaves or female serfs of noble and powerful gentlemen, in order to escape the demands of their rank under the protection of their new masters. In short, any and every means to this end was employed, and, though they might often fail, another time they might come off. This leading stratum of the population of the cities, then, regularly used the weapons of deceit and bribery against the might of the State, and, in the end, both parties in the quarrel lost their stake. There is no need to emphasize how disastrous all this was for the morale of the whole people. The bold and ingenious spent all their acumen in finding new ways of evading the law. Many ruined themselves in gaining the protection of powerful advocates, and all to no purpose. Even if fortune smiled on you, you lived in perpetual fear that the Emperor might change his attitude all of a sudden and put you back in your old rank. Anyone, then, who came of the class of decurions, and had won an official position, must, as far as possible, keep his origin a secret. He must always be pretending and lying, if he was to escape the danger that threatened him.'[1]

The laws of Constantine[2] already show us authoritatively that these evil conditions were ripe at the beginning of the century.

We have spent some time in describing the abuses connected with the decurions; but that does not mean that conditions were better in other orders of society. The whole of the Roman Empire in its decline was dominated by the blind lust for gold.[3] If we look first at that army of officials that from the time of Diocletian had grown to such enormous size, we find that nothing could be done with it without baksheesh.[4] If you refused it, you were not even brought into court; the senior official abused his seniority to squeeze money from the litigants; you had especially to bribe lavishly the persons who dispatched the official drafts.[5] Even at the beginning of the

[1] O. Seeck, op. cit., pp. 330 ff.

[2] For example, *Cod. Theod.* xvi. 3. 6. 7.

[3] Rutil. Namat. 1. 358 ff.: 'auri caecus amor ducit in omne nefas; Aurea legitimas expugnant munera taedas Virgineosque sinus aureus imber emit, Auro victa fides munitas decipit urbes, Auri flagitiis ambitus ipse furit.'

[4] E. Bethmann-Hollweg, *Der Zivilprozess*, iii, 1886, 200.

[5] *Cod. Theod.* i. 16. 7.

century officials were regarded as so many leeches.[1] As we turn
the pages of the late Roman legislation we meet an infinite
series of edicts against the extortions of the bureaux. Many
attempts were made to effect a radical cure. Julian, for example, discharged a large number of greedy subordinates out
of hand.[2] Later, the Pannonian Viventius, *praefectus praetorio
Galliarum*, made another great clearance, which won the en-
thusiastic approval of Valentinian.[3] But it was all in vain; the
thousand heads of the hydra grew again as fast as they were
cut off.

Even when we look at the higher spheres, the picture that
meets us is still comfortless. Diocletian himself had placed his
governors under strict control. 'On every side he kept them
under check—from above by the *praefectus praetorio* and his
vicarius, from the side by the provincial military commander
(*dux*) and his financial officials, from below by his own bureaux,
directed by a professional chicaner.' But it is a matter of
experience that, when a corps of civil servants has become
thoroughly corrupt, such measures are only effective as long
as they are fresh. As soon as the civil servants have become at
home with the regulations, they at once discover the crooked
ways by which they can evade their effects. This was already
the case under Constantine, and, after him, when there were
far more hungry mouths to be stopped with gold, the oppression of the subjects went from bad to worse.[4] At first the governors were controlled by special emissaries, later by the *notarii*
and *palatini*.[5] In the age of the sons of Constantine it was the
so-called *agentes in rebus*, whom everyone hated and before
whom everyone crawled, 'the ubiquitous spies', who had grown
to be a veritable plague.[6] Besides their other duties they extorted money over the whole Empire, as the heralds of the
victories and joyful festivities of the imperial house.[7] Corrup-

---

[1] Ibid.

[2] See e.g. J. Bidez, *La Vie de l'empereur Julien*, 1930, 213 ff., 242 ff.; J.
Geffcken, *Kaiser Iulianus*, 1914, 62 ff.; W. Ensslin, *Klio*, xviii, 1922, 103 ff.;
R. Andreoti, *Nuova Riv. Stor.* xiv, 1930, 342 ff.

[3] *Cod. Theod.* viii. 7. 10.   [4] O. Seeck, op. cit. ii. 281 ff. and 101 ff.

[5] Ibid. 81 ff., 83.

[6] Ibid. 95 ff., 98 ff.; cf. Seeck, *RE*. i. 777.

[7] Id., *Gesch. d. Unt. d. ant. Welt*, ii. 104 f.

tion grew hand over fist.[1] By the end of the century official fraud
was punishable with death,[2] in order to put a break on abuses.
But of course it was all in vain.

The Imperial Court itself was not much better. Ammianus
describes the courtiers of Constantius II as 'a hotbed of all
vices' (*vitiorum omnium seminarium*). In the twinkling of an
eye they would assemble a vast fortune by deceit and violence,
only to waste their days in revelry and debauch, to parade
their magnificent clothes and build grand palaces.[3] Even if
Constantius only nominated men to the higher ranks after
thorough consideration and selection, all his care was wasted.[4]

Julian, it is true, imposed a severe discipline on this horde
of bandits;[5] but we ought probably to apply to him the phrase
that the malicious applied to Titus, son of Vespasian, 'the
darling of the human race'—but only 'darling' because he died
after a mercifully short reign. Even Julian could never in the
end have mastered the disease; it was only his sudden death
that created the illusion that he might have done so. In any
case it is hard to see how, after him, Valentinian could be held
responsible[6] for those desperate conditions, which he had inherited from his predecessors, and against which he fought
tooth and nail.[7]

Corruption at this time, then, was very great, and it grew
with the steady deterioration of conditions, with the incessant
wars and the vast works of frontier defence.[8] Ammianus, for
example, has given us a horrifying sketch of the ill deeds of one
officer in high rank and of the way in which his kinsman,
Remigius, who held the high position of *magister officii* at court,
contrived to delude the Emperor, so that the iron fist of

---

[1] Cf., for example, the Edict of Valens, addressed to a *proconsul Asiae*,
discussed by A. Schulten, *Jahreshefte d. Österr. Arch. Inst.* ix, 1906, 192.

[2] *Cod. Theod.* ix. 28. 1.   [3] Ammianus xxii. 4. 2–5.

[4] Seeck, op. cit. iv. 33 ff.

[5] W. Ensslin, op. cit.; R. Andreotti, op. cit.

[6] By Seeck, op. cit. v. 14 and by E. Stein, *Gesch. d. spätröm. Reiches*, i, 1928,
275 ff.

[7] Cf., for example, A. Nagl, *RE.* vii A. 2189 ff.

[8] Zosimus iv. 16. 1. On the frontier defences see also my remarks in *Der
Untergang der Römerherrschaft in Pannonien*, i, 1924, 76 ff.; A. Nagl, *RE.*
vii A. 2193 f.

Valentinian struck the innocent instead of the guilty: I mean the notorious case of Romanus,[1] who had probably been appointed *comes Africae* already under Jovian.[2]

The opponents of Pope Damasus asserted that he had bought up the whole Court,[3] and, even if the story is not true, the mere fact that such rumours could be disseminated throws a lurid light on general conditions. The author of an official panegyric to Valens tells him outright, as a fact generally acknowledged, how corrupt things are,[4] and the continuous succession of new imperial edicts reflects the same picture. In the sequel, the general tone in such matters grew steadily worse. Of the Court of Gratian, it was not unjustly observed that you could buy anything there for gold.[5]

The collapse of the Danube *limes* and the terrible devastations of the Germans, Alans, and Huns abetted in their mischief all the extortioners and cheats who fished in those troubled waters.[6] Perhaps we ought not to take quite literally the biting satires of a Claudius Claudianus on the two confidants of Theodosius, the *praefectus praetorio*, Rufinus, and the chief chamberlain, the eunuch Eutropius; but the glorious flow of his verse gives us a very vivid and telling picture of the sins of the Court.[7] The laws kept on threatening offenders with punishments that became ever more terrifying, but they effected no cure.[8]

This spirit of corruption was not, of course, confined to civil

---

[1] Ammianus xxvii. 9. 1–3, xxviii. 6. 15 ff., xxx. 2. 9–12.

[2] Seeck, *RE*. i A. 1065.

[3] 'Quae gesta sunt inter Liberium et Felicem episcopos', cf. 11 (*Corp. Script. Eccl. Lat.* xxxv. 4): 'redemit omne palatium'.

[4] Themist. *or.* p. 135. 33 ff. Dind.

[5] Sulp. Sev. *chron.* ii. 49. 3: 'quia per libidinem et potentiam paucorum cuncta ibi venalia erant'.

[6] Just one example; Paulinus, *Vita Ambr.* 41: 'ingemiscebat enim vehementer cum videret radicem omnium vitiorum avaritiam pullulare, quae . . . magis magisque increscere in hominibus, et maxime iis, qui in potestatibus erant constituti; ita ut interveniendi illi apud illos gravissimus labor esset, quia omnia pretio distrahebantur'.

[7] In his poem addressed to his patron, Stilicho, Claudianus writes (*De cons. Stil.* ii. 116 ff.): 'nec te gurges corruptior aevi Traxit ad exemplum qui iam firmaverat annis Crimen et in legem rapiendi verterat usum'.

[8] A characteristic example in *Cod. Theod.* ix. 27. 6.

D

life. The army too was deeply tainted by it. Commanders embezzled the pay of their troops, allotted them less corn than they had received on their behalf, and went on to sell what they had thus saved; as a result, their men stole and robbed the small landowners of the neighbourhood of their necessary means of livelihood.[1]

We have seen clearly in the case of Petronius Probus how even the sons of the great landowners were not free from the general lust for gold and how the crooked paths of avarice were familiar to them.[2] The ways in which these cultured gentlemen raked in the shekels were not as crude as those of the others,[3] but they are equally indefensible—as indefensible as the acts of violence on the part of these great lords by which they contributed to the ruin of the State. We are thinking, in particular, of the way in which the poor peasants—if they could not sneak into the city to beg their living, or escape to the mountains as bandits—would surrender their small rights of property to some powerful landlord or other, who then defended them against the tax-collector.[4]

The influence of the families of Roman magnates on administration steadily grew. The chief reason for this was that it became easier and easier to gain the higher posts by bribery or, it might be, by purchase,[5] and they had plenty of money for the purpose.

Constantine himself had been up in arms against the attempts of the decurions to gain admission to administrative posts, releasing them from their obligations,[6] by patronage for which

[1] Themist. *or*. 10. 136 A–C; Zosimus iv. 27. 3; Liban. *or*. 2. 37 ff., 47. 9 ff., 13, 17, 29 ff.; R. A. Pack, *Studies in Libanius and Antiochene Society under Theodosius*, Diss. Michigan, 1935, 15 ff.

[2] Cf. also what Ammianus (xxvii. 7. 2) writes about Vulcacius Rufinus, the predecessor of Probus: 'Vulcacius Rufinus omni ex parte perfectus et velut apicem senectutis honoratae praetendens, sed lucrandi opportunas occasiones occultationis spe numquam praetermittens'.

[3] See Note 8, p. 129.

[4] Seeck, *Gesch. d. Unt. d. ant. Welt.* ii². 297 ff. We shall come back in a later chapter to the part played by the aristocracy. Cf. F. Martroye in *Revue d'Hist. d. droit*, 4ᵉ sér. vii, 1928, 201 ff.; A. Piganiol, op. cit. 360 ff. (n. 98 literature on the subject).   [5] Cf. Seeck, op. cit. ii². 61.

[6] *Cod. Theod.* vi. 22. 1.

they had paid. His sons continued his fight after his death,[1] Julian issued general edicts against men who bought their offices.[2] A *constitutio* of Valentinian brands such abuses on the part of subordinate officials.[3] And what we have is only a small fraction of all the edicts that accidentally survives. But the criminal practices kept on spreading and rising into higher and higher spheres. Under Theodosius the Court allots governorships to all kinds of parvenus, who then aim at recouping themselves for their expenditure from those whose interests they ought in duty to protect.[4] The same tale is repeated again and again in the following generations.[5]

The rich aristocratic families bought for their young sons posts that, in the good old days, had only been held by men of mature age.[6] The administration of the Late Empire, with its mechanical routine, no longer rested on the suitability of its leaders, but depended on the trained and experienced officers of the Chancellory. That was why the nominal control could be exercised by one who was little more than a child.

The most alarming symptom was that, as the State recognized as legal income the moneys paid over to its officials for breaches of the law and only attempted to train its men to accept a moderate tariff,[7] the sums paid in bribery to obtain a post were also legalized. The State was now ready to exploit the possibilities of this lucrative source of income for itself. As early as Constans (A.D. 337–50) our authorities maintain that the Emperor himself sold provincial governorships for cash;[8] and, even if this disgraceful practice ceased for a time under his successors—the reign of Valentinian was completely free of

---

[1] Ibid. vi. 22. 2; xii. 1. 25–7. [2] Ibid. ii. 29. 1.
[3] Ibid. viii. 4. 10. [4] Zosimus iv. 28. 2–29. 2.
[5] Salvian. *De gubern. Dei*, iv. 4. 21.
[6] Cf. the quotations which Seeck appends to his observations in *Gesch. d. Unt. d. ant. Welt*, ii². 101. [7] Seeck, op. cit. ii². 103 ff.
[8] *Epit. de Caes.* 41. 24: 'quae profecto maiora fierent, si provinciarum rectores non pretio sed iudicio provexisset'. Seeck has already observed that the comment in Victor, *Caes.*, on Constans (41. 23), 'praeceps in avaritiam', may have the same meaning; the late Roman writers regularly class the exploitation of the subjects by the Emperor under the heading of *avaritia*, understanding by the word not passive covetousness but active grasping; so, too, in the case of Valentinian.

it[1]—yet, towards the close of the century especially under Theodosius, it broke out with renewed virulence.[2] At the beginning of the fifth century the practice was so much taken for granted that the higher dignities were classified as either won by merit or by money.[3] Contemporaries set this abuse down to the score of the Empress, Pulcheria[4]—but only because they were unaware of the older abuses that we have mentioned. We get the impression that even the most brilliant distinction of the Empire, the ordinary consulship, was not given only to men who had grown grey in honourable service, but was also for sale. Otherwise, the two young and immature sons of the Petronius Probus who died in A.D. 395, Olybrius and Probinus, and many others could hardly have obtained it.[5]

The pressure of imperial omnipotence, that now rises to the pitch of brutal caprice, could only accelerate the increase of corruption; the increase of corruption, on the other hand, aggravated the brutality with which the Government tried to punish it. The blows and counterblows that followed in regular succession accelerated the process of decay. As we turn the pages of the legislation of the *Codex Theodosianus*, we are horrified as we read the appalling nature of the punishments. Interrogation with its instruments of torture is an everyday matter. The knout tears strips out of the back of the accused till the blood pours down in torrents.[6] In the cramped cells of the prisons, where food was of the scantiest and where the jailer had to be handsomely bribed to provide a pitiful oil-lamp, the prisoners were tormented and beaten, and died like

[1] Ammianus xxx. 9. 3: 'scrupulosus in deferendis potestatibus celsis, nec imperante eo provinciam nummularius rexit, aut administratio venundata'.

[2] Zosimus iv. 28. 3 ff.

[3] *Cod. Theod.* vi. 18. 1 (A.D. 412, 15 Oct.): he who 'primi ordinis comitivam aut pretio impetravit aut gratia' stands in the order of rank behind those who have received office for merit.

[4] Eunap. frg. 79 Boiss. (*Exc. de sent.*, p. 100).

[5] Such a lad, for example, might be Rufinus Praetextatus Postumianus, *praefectus urbi secundo* and *consul ordinarius* in A.D. 448, the son of the ordinary consul of A.D. 423, who, according to the inscription (*C.I.L.* vi. 1761 = *I.L.S.* 1285) 'quos tantos ac tales honores primo aetatis suae flore promeruit'.

[6] A. Ehrhardt, *RE*. vi A. 1775 ff., gives the rest of the literature.

flies from their awful sufferings.[1] Among punishments the death penalty is a commonplace, among the methods of execution burning alive is normal, not to mention other horrors that raise the hair.[2]

Men of culture had plenty to say about their *humanitas*, φιλανθρωπία;[3] even the Emperors had never been so eloquent about their untroubled repose (*tranquillitas nostra*), their mercy (*mansuetudo nostra*), and their pious serenity (*serenitas nostra*), as in the fourth century and later. But such self-praise carries no weight;[4] the choice words are a mere empty form, which only seek to disguise the sad fact that law has become an iron fetter, the hand of the Emperor a butcher's axe.

In such an atmosphere the Emperor, the source and supreme executor of the law, appears as a veritable shape of terror.[5] Listen to the furious outbreak of Constantine in one of his edicts:[6]

'Cease, now, at once, you greedy hands of my officials, cease, I bid you. For if, after this warning, you do not cease, the sword shall hew you off. The zeal of the governor must ever be on the watch, to see that none of such men as have been mentioned [the *officiales*], shall accept a bribe from a litigant. For, if they presume to demand anything in civil cases armed vengeance will be at hand to sever the hand and neck of the shameful offender. But, if he [the governor] chooses to shut his

[1] Liban. *or.* 45, vol. 3, p. 359 (Foerster).

[2] Mommsen, *Röm. Strafrecht*, 1899, 911 ff.; E. Costa, *Crimini e pene da Romolo a Giustiniano*, 1921.

[3] R. A. Pack, *Studies in Libanius and Antiochene Society*, Diss. Michigan, 1935, 70 ff.

[4] The prelude to an edict of Valentinian of the year A.D. 371–2 may serve as characteristic (*Epist. imper.* 11 = *Corp. Script. Eccl. Lat.* xxxv, p. 52): 'iure mansuetudinis nostrae sensibus vel divinitus datum est vel tranquillitate naturae, ne cum delinquentium facinore legum severitate certemus ac spe emendationis futurae mitiorem esse velimus correctionis iniuriam quam provocat meritum noxiorum, Ampeli parens carissime atque amantissime'. Cf. ibid. *ep.* 12 (*Corp. Script. Eccl. Lat.* xxxv, p. 53).

[5] Ammianus xxvi. 2. 11, on the newly elected Valentinian: 'circumsaeptum aquilis et vexillis, agminibusque diversorum ordinum ambitiose stipatum, iamque terribilem duxerunt in regiam'. In the idea that men formed of the Emperor, the *adorandum* stood very close to the *tremendum*, as it does in the world of religious emotion.

[6] *Cod. Theod.* i. 16. 7.

eyes, we permit every man to accuse him . . . in order that we may impose the death penalty on all such robberies.'

This attitude of arbitrary intimidation is not peculiar to Constantine; it is more or less characteristic of all his successors.

Even scholars often forget how blood-stained were the hands of most Emperors of this century. The legislation of Constantine was not as much mitigated by Christianity as is ordinarily supposed.[1] Heavy on his soul lay the deaths, not only of his father-in-law, Herculius, and his brother-in-law, Licinius, but also those of his son, Crispus, and his wife, Fausta. It need hardly be observed that his massacres were by no means restricted to the executions of those members of the imperial family whom we have mentioned.[2] But, whereas, in Constantine, the bestial anger that would suddenly wake in him is easier to understand and the sobriety that always followed quickly after and his sincere penitence for his sins have a more human aspect, the cold, deliberate, hypocritical cruelty of his son, Constantius II, is all the more repellent by contrast.[3] It is quite clear that Constantius had his own share in the horrors of A.D. 337, when two sisters of his father, six nephews, and his father's confidant, Ablabius, were murdered. He was present at the scene of their deaths, and he approved of them by confiscating the property of his kin.[4] Even in later years, his conscience was burdened by a series of common murders.[5] And how many more were brought to destruction by the bloodhounds of that scoundrelly despotism, the notorious Paulus, *notarius*, the *agens in rebus* Apodemius, and hundreds upon hundreds of their companions

---

[1] G. Costa, *Religione e politica nell' impero Romano*, 1923, 257 ff.

[2] Cf., for example, Eutrop. x. 6. 3.

[3] Ammianus xxi. 16. 8–9: 'Caligulae et Domitiani et Commodi immanitatem facile superabat, . . . mortemque longius in puniendis quibusdam, si natura permitteret, conabatur extendi'. Compare with this the words of Mamertinus (*Grat. act.* 26): 'quis nescit aliorum imperatorum hilarem diritatem cacchinantemque saevitiam? a quibus ingenita crudelitas figmento laetitiae tegebatur'.

[4] According to E. Stein (*Gesch.* i. 203) 'he was in a position of duress in face of rebellious adherents'; in this point he shares the view of Olivetti, *Riv. di filol.* xliii, 1915, 67 ff. This I regard as too simple-minded; cf. also Seeck, *Gesch. d. Unt. d. ant. Welt*, iv. 28 ff.

[5] The details are given, for example, by Seeck, op. cit. iv. 36, 119, 133.

in crime! The Caesar, Gallus, co-regent of Constantius, committed similar horrible acts of cruelty and it was often the childish suspicion of magic that drove him to them.[1] Even the most moderate of all the Emperors, Julian, ordered the execution of some of the confidants of his predecessor,[2] the innocent together with the guilty.[3]

Horrible, indeed, was the treatment meted out by the elder Theodosius, the father of the Emperor, to the rebels in North Africa.[4] But Ammianus uses a different tone in speaking of him, the ancestor of the reigning dynasty, from that which he applies to Valentinian, the enemy of his dear Roman aristocrats, when, in their spirit, he brands him after his death as a brutal tyrant. If he ventures to describe the elder Theodosius as a rough and 'bloodthirsty' man, as an 'inventor of new death penalties' (*truculentus et dirus et suppliciorum novorum saevus repertor*,[5] it is only by putting the words into the mouth of a rebel. He even quotes Cicero in excuse of his awful bloodletting: 'salutary severity surpasses the empty show of forgiving mercy'.[6] But Theodosius, the son, outdid his father. Among the brutish massacres which, in his case, were followed by sudden collapses, the blood-bath of Thessalonica is the best known. In revenge for the killing of one of his generals, a German, Theodosius ordered a massacre of the people, assembled in the circus, in which many thousands perished; but, in the sequel, he broke down completely and, in humblest obedience to Bishop Ambrose, did penance for his crime. How men trembled before his anger is shown by the case of the people of Antioch. Having once kindled his fury, they fled out of their city, neck and crop, to escape extermination.[7] There

---

[1] Ammianus xiv. 1. 2: 'artium nefandarum calumniae'. It is nothing less than a miracle if anyone is acquitted on a charge of magic: Ammianus xiv. 7. 7 ff.

[2] Ibid. xxii. 3. 1 ff.; Sozom. v. 5. Cf. E. A. Thompson, op. cit. 73 ff.

[3] Even the short reign of Jovian was not free from such acts: Ammianus xxv. 8. 18, xxvi. 6. 3.

[4] Ibid. xxix. 5. 22–4.

[5] Ibid. 48. Cf. now also E. A. Thompson, op. cit. 89 f., 93 ff., 97 ff., 106.

[6] See Note 9, p. 130.

[7] A. Rauschen, *Jahrbücher d. christl. Kirche*, 1897, 259 ff.

are still more examples of bloody savagery like this that might be quoted.[1]

Cruelty of this order cannot fully be explained by the corruption of the age, which could only be in some measure suppressed by blood and iron; the spirit of the fourth century has its part to play. The victory of abstract ways of thinking, the universal triumph of theory, knows no half-measures; punishment, like everything else, must be a hundred per cent., but even this seemed to be inadequate.

The less specialized observer will be helped to understand how the mechanical methods gained the upper hand over the organic conception of treatment, if he will reflect on the distinction between the surgeon and the physician in internal disorders. To take an example: the weather is bad, a child is feverish and its tonsils need to be removed. The physician is afraid of possible complications after the operation that may endanger the organism. The surgeon is quite unconcerned about the consequences of the removal of the tonsils—his concern is with the life of his patient. The more acute the danger, the heavier does this consideration weigh. We can trace a conflict like this over the persecutions of the Christians in the third century. The Church, in the view of the Roman State, was a foreign growth, of serious proportions, in the social organism, feared as dangerous to the collective life of the world. As such, most Emperors wished to remove it by an operation on the body politic. But the sequel proved that they were wrong and that the gentle treatment of symptoms, involved in the policy of Gallienus, would have done more good.[2] In times of crisis, when the choice of the Government is simplified down to a plain 'to be or not to be', the policy that wins is that of the fire-brigade, which elects to destroy the contents of a house in order to save the naked walls. That the internal decay of the second half of the fourth century—to retain our medical metaphor—had become as bad as a cancerous growth can certainly not be questioned.

The rapid increase of the Terror was also assisted by the

[1] Cf., for example, Seeck, *Gesch. d. Unt. d. ant. Welt*, v. 170 ff., 175, 229 ff.
[2] A. Alföldi, *Klio*, xxxi, 1938, 323 ff.; and 25. *Jahre röm.-germ. Komm.* 1929, 17 ff.

atmosphere of growing barbarism, when soldiers, ruling with iron fist, sat on the throne—men like Constantine, Valentinian, and Theodosius; but the second of the three was not a 'passionate man of blood'.[1] The description is far better applicable to the other two.

We have already stressed the fact that such a conception of Valentinian is nothing but an echo of the prejudiced and exaggerated sketch of his character given us by Ammianus Marcellinus, that supreme historian of late Rome who, in the great clash of wills that we have still to describe, stood, body and soul, on the side of the senators—and so against the Emperor. When Ammianus records the bloody sentences passed by Valentinian[2] he is certainly thinking of those examinations of scions of the noble Roman families under torture which infuriated the whole aristocracy; we need not suppose that the tortures which the lesser folk had to endure troubled him in the least. As a normal part of legal proceeding they were matter-of-course under every Emperor of the age. The one-sided accounts which Ammianus permits himself to give of the bloody cruelties of our Emperor are first of all connected with the criminal proceedings against the Roman nobles.[3] Ammianus states in so many words that he regards these Bloody Assizes against the privileged notables as an injustice that cries to heaven.[4] He talks as if nothing like it had ever occurred before; and yet he himself records that Constantius II in similar cases had unhesitatingly done the same.[5] He even admits in another context— no doubt in loyalty to the Emperor of his own time—that according to the spirit of the *leges Corneliae*, in cases of attacks

[1] As Seeck, op. cit. v. 41, states.   [2] Ammianus xxx. 8. 3.

[3] Ibid. xxviii. 1. 20, 23, 26 and 2. 9.

[4] Ibid. xxviii. 1. 11: Valentinian allows Maximinus to interrogate the *viri clarissimi* under torture: 'uno proloquio, in huiusmodi causas, quas adroganter proposito maiestatis imminutae miscebat, omnes quos iuris prisci iustitia, divorumque arbitria, quaestionibus exemere cruentis, si postulasset negotium, statuit tormentis adfligi'.

[5] Ibid. xix. 12. 9: 'ductus est itaque inter primos Simplicius Philippi filius, ex praefecto et consule, reus hac gratia postulatus, quod super adipiscendo interrogasse dicebatur imperio, perque elogium principis torqueri praeceptus, qui in his casibus nec peccatum aliquando pietati dederat, nec erratum, fato quodam arcente, corpore inmaculato lata fuga damnatus est'.

or attempted attacks, endangering the life of the Emperor, the privileged exemption from examination under torture was suspended for each and every class of society.[1] Nor could he fail to realize that it was just those acts of magic and witchcraft that were the chief substance of the *causes célèbres* at Rome that we have mentioned, which were punished with such horrible forms of execution by the predecessors and successors of Valentinian.[2]

The malice of Ammianus is revealed especially clearly when he narrates in detail the bloodthirsty orders which Valentinian issued in his fury, only to revoke them immediately after,[3] or when he gives his assent to childish stories of horror, like that of the pet bears that ate human flesh, which Valentinian, in sheer fury, allowed to tear some of his victims to pieces.[4] In other points we might prove in detail that our illustrious historian has been looking at Valentinian through a distorting mirror.[5] Often he seems to feel himself that he has been overshooting the mark.[6]

If we carefully remove, piece by piece, the lurid web which hatred has spun about the memory of Valentinian, the picture of the 'passionate man of blood', of the blood-sucking monster of O. Seeck, dissolves in the mists of fancy. That Valentinian was, by nature, passionate is beyond all doubt,[7] however much

---

[1] Ammianus xix. 12. 17–18: 'et inquisitum in haec negotia fortius nemo qui quidem recte sapiat, reprehendet. nec enim abnuimus salutem legitimi principis, propugnatoris bonorum et defensoris, unde salus quaeritur aliis, consociato studio muniri debere cunctorum; cuius retinendae causa validius, ubi maiestas pulsata defenditur, a quaestionibus vel cruentis nullam Corneliae leges exemere fortunam. sed exultare maestis casibus effrenate non decet, ne videantur licentia regi subiecti non potestate'.

[2] Cf. below. It is enough here to quote a few of the Draconian laws of Theodosius: *Cod. Theod.* xvi. 10. 9 and 12, ibid. ix. 16. 1 ff.

[3] See Note 10, p. 130.   [4] See Note 11, p. 131.

[5] See Note 12, p. 131.

[6] After recounting examples of the cruelty of Valentinian, Ammianus writes (xxix. 3. 9): 'horrescit animus omnia recensere, simulque reformidat, ne ex professo quaesisse videamur in vitia principis, alia commodissimi'. But a little later (4. 1) we read: 'et haec quidem morum eius et propositi cruenti sunt documenta verissima. sollertiae vero circa rem publicam usquam digredientis, nemo eum vel obtrectator pervicax incusabit'.

[7] Ibid. xxx. 5. 3: 'acer et vehemens'.

he tried to control himself.[1] It was in his angry excitement, when he scornfully abused the peace embassy of the German Quadi, who had been devastating Pannonia, that his stroke smote him.[2] Outbreaks of fury on the part of the master of millions may often have had serious consequences; once, for example, Valentinian, on the hunt, ordered a young man (one of his courtiers) to be put to death because he had released the hunting-dogs under his charge too soon and had thus disturbed the drive.[3] But what is an act like that, dreadful though it is, in comparison to the horrible massacres of close relatives by Constantine or the mass butcheries of Theodosius? Aurelian was nicknamed 'hand-on-hilt' (*manu ad ferrum*), and the rest of the Illyrian generals and Emperors, mostly of peasant stock, may have been as rough in their behaviour: Valentinian, though his father before him had held a high rank, represents just the same type of man.

His hands were clean of blood when he mounted the throne, and after that he never abused his exalted position. His self-control is again illustrated by his spotless family life and is also reflected in his conduct towards his kindred, which from the point of view of the common weal must be pronounced correct; further, in the discipline of his Court, which, by the standards of the age, was strict.[4] In spite of his sullen exterior,[5] he was not lacking in a kindly moderation,[6] and it is just this moderation that lifts him high above Constantine, who had superior powers of imagination, but less control of his moral brakes, or above Theodosius, whose judgement was variable and who

---

[1] See Note 13, p. 132.

[2] Ammianus xxx. 6. 3; Socrat. iv. 31. 4–5; Zosimus iv. 17. 2, &c.

[3] Ammianus xxix. 3. 3. One is reminded of the story of Hadrian, who in anger threw his pen in the eye of a poor slave, in Galen, vol. xviii, p. 18 Kühn.

[4] Ammianus xxx. 9. 2: 'omni pudicitiae cultu domi castus et foris, nullo contagio conscientiae violatus obscenae, nihil incestum: hancque ob causam tamquam retinaculis petulantiam frenarat aulae regalis, quod custodire facile potuit, necessitudinibus suis nihil indulgens, quas aut in otio reprimebat, aut mediocriter honoravit, absque fratre, quem temporis compulsus angustiis, in amplitudinis suae societatem adsumpsit'.

[5] Ibid. xxx. 9. 6: 'semper obliquum intuentis et torvum'.

[6] See Note 14, p. 132.

was again and again carried away by his impressions and passions.[1] Even Constantius II would never have acted as Valentinian did to his *magister memoriae*, Rusticus Iulianus, and his *magister peditum* Severus in A.D. 367.[2] They had actually been designated as his successors at the time of his serious illness and, yet, after his recovery, he did not touch a hair of their heads, but allowed the normal advance of their careers.[3]

The self-control of Valentinian is further shown in the fact that he immediately revokes the punishments that he has imposed in his anger when his courtiers appeal to him,[4] that he gives in to their pleadings when they venture to express opinions contrary to his[5] or even to correct his mistakes.[6] The loveliest and noblest evidence of his moderation is seen in his religious policy, with which we shall have to deal fully later.

The iron severity of this disciplined soldier was, then, no mere outbreak of blind anger, but was based on many other causes and was only in a smaller degree dependent on his individual temper.

For one thing, the public spirit of old Rome demanded a hard and bitter seriousness in matters of discipline and punishment. This *severitas* often figures among the virtues of the old *imperatores*.[7] For another, the old principle of severity was reinforced, in this late Roman age, by the alarming growth of compulsion in all walks of life and by what appears to us as the appalling harshness of the punishment with which the general corruption was to be checked. It helped little that Valentinian, from the top of his head to the tip of his toes, was decent, that he was

---

[1] Themistius too (*or.* 9, p. 150. 26 ff. Dind.) praises the moderate conduct of Valentinian.

[2] Ammianus xxvii. 6. 1–2.

[3] Seeck, *Symm.*, p. cxxv and *Die Briefe d. Libanius*, 1906, 274.

[4] See Note 15, p. 132.

[5] So, for example, his general, Dagalaifus (Ammianus xxvi. 4. 1), who, on the occasion of the choice of the second Emperor, gave him his opinion unvarnished and yet received the highest distinctions from Valentinian (Seeck, *RE*. iv. 1984).   [6] Ammianus xxviii. 1. 25.

[7] Of course malice could not apply epithets like *acerbus, truculentus* to an Emperor, whom well-wishers called *severus*, without some reason. Ammianus always stresses this dark side of the severity of our Emperor. Cf., for example, xxviii. 1. 11: 'ut erat vitiorum inimicus acer magis quam severus'.

permeated by a sense of justice.[1] His military roughness and his inexorable logic only heightened the pressure of this merciless age. The prescriptions of the criminal law were, as we have observed, severe enough in themselves; but Valentinian demanded that they should be administered by the strictest standards,[2] and, when appeal was made to him, did not mitigate the punishments assigned, but even in some cases increased them.[3]

The charge that Valentinian reserved this terrifying severity for the small man and shut his eyes to the sins of the great[4] cannot be sustained.[5] For example, when he discovered that Petronius Probus, the all-powerful prefect, was abusing his trust, it was only death that prevented him from requiting his misdeeds.[6] Diocles, the former *comes sacrarum largitionum*, was

[1] See Note 16, p. 133.

[2] Ammianus xxx. 8. 13: 'ut noxas vel leves acerbius vindicarent'. Cf. xxviii. 1. 22 ff.

[3] Ibid. xxx. 8. 13–14, xxx. 8. 3: 'nec enim usquam repperitur miti cohercitione contentus, sed aliquotiens quaestiones multiplicari iussisse cruentas, per interrogationes funestas, non nullis ad usque discrimina vitae vexatis: et ita erat effusior ad nocendum, ut nullum aliquando damnatorum capitis eriperet morte subscriptionis elogio leni, cum id etiam principes interdum fecere saevissimi'. xxx. 8. 6: 'minimeque reputans adflicti solacium status semper esse lenitudinem principum, poenas per ignes augebat et gladios'. Cf. xxviii. 1. 26 and 44; Zosimus iv. 2. 4.

[4] Ammianus xxvii. 9. 4: 'indeflexa saevitia punientem gregariorum errata, parcentem potioribus'; xxx. 5. 3: 'et quamquam terrori cunctis erat dum sperabatur, ut acer et vehemens, mox iudices damnari iussurus, quorum perfidia vel secessione Pannoniarum nudatum latus; cum illuc venisset, ita intepuit, ut neque in Gabinii regis inquireret necem, neque iniusta reipublicae vulnera, quo sinente vel agente, segnius evenissent, curatius vestigaret: eo videlicet more, quo erat severus in gregariis corrigendis, remissior erga maiores fortunas, vel verbis asperioribus incessendas'.

[5] Cf., on the other hand, Zonaras xiii. 15. 4–6 (p. 73 Büttner-Wobst): διὸ καὶ τῶν ἀρχὰς τότε μετιόντων πολλοὺς ὡς ἀδίκους ἐτιμωρήσατο, τὸν κρατοῦντα λέγων ἀπαιτεῖσθαι δικαιοσύνης πρὸ τῶν ἄλλων, φροντίζειν; Ioh. Antioch. frg. 182 (*F.H.G.* iv. 607 = *Exc. de virt.*, p. 201 de Boor): πρὸς δὲ ταῖς τῶν ἀρχόντων αἱρέσεσιν ἀκριβὴς καὶ τιμωρὸς τῶν ἀπειθούντων ἀπαραίτητος; *Chron. pasch.* a. 369.

[6] Ammianus xxx. 5. 4: 'solum tamen incitato petebat odio Probum, numquam ex quo eum viderat, minari desinens vel mitescens'; 10: 'in immensum excanduit' (when he heard of the scandalous government of Probus) 'urente irarum nutrimenta tunc magistro Leone . . . ipso quoque praefecturam . . . adfectante'.

burned alive for a comparatively small offence,[1] and another of his favourites, Rhodanus, suffered the same fate for defrauding a widow.[2] An *agens in rebus*, Diodorus, was put to death with three minor officials for a mere trifle,[3] as was also a provincial governor.[4] Two high officers of the guard were punished with death or banishment because they had agitated in the interest of the rebel, Procopius.[5] The director of a State factory for arms dedicated a splendid cuirass to Valentinian; but, when it came out that the silver overlay was somewhat under the prescribed weight, instead of reward the man received the death sentence, which was then imposed for quite minor frauds.[6]

It is not surprising that Valentinian should show even less concern for the small folk, whose lives, in the opinion of the time, were far cheaper than those of the nobles. A subordinate officer, who had exchanged the horses which he had to take over for the army for inferior ones, was stoned to death at his orders.[7] A popular charioteer, who came under suspicion of a similar fraud and was further accused of secret intrigues, was ordered to be burned alive.[8]

It was not so bad as long as the awful severity with which Valentinian tried to further the welfare of his peoples fell on

[1] Ammianus xxvii. 7. 5.

[2] Ioh. Antioch. frg. 183 (*F.H.G.* iv. 607); Eunap. frg. 30 (*F.H.G.* iv. 26); *Chron. pasch.* a. 369; Malal. xiii, p. 340 Bonn; cf. Suidas, s.v. προθέματα.

[3] From the report of Ammianus (xxvii. 7. 5) it becomes clear that this was generally regarded as an act of injustice; that it happened in Milan provides us with a date; it can only have taken place at the beginning of the reign, from autumn A.D. 364 to autumn 365 or in A.D. 374.

[4] Ammianus (xxix. 3. 6) certainly misrepresents the facts. For this Africanus could never have suffered any kind of punishment for trying to become governor of another province and seeking the help of the elder Theodosius in his aim.

[5] Ibid. xxix. 3. 7. Characteristic of his tone is the fact that he does not think that any such severe judgement should have been passed—just because the plaintiff was a small man of no importance ('accusabat quidam vilitate ipsa despectus').   [6] See Note 17, p. 133.

[7] Ammianus xxix. 3. 5.

[8] Ammianus (ibid.) on this occasion is no doubt moved by prejudice when he laments this *artifex voluptatum*; the people too used to rage at the misfortunes of its favourites. In general, Ammianus despises wholeheartedly the amusements and passions of the idle plebs (xiv. 6. 25–6) and is well aware that *veneficium* was punishable with death by torture.

sinners. But we begin to shudder when the Emperor is deluded by corrupt courtiers and when his blood harshness overtakes the innocent. There was one case when a kinsman of Valentinian and the judges whom he had bribed hushed up the scandalous misdeeds of a military commander and when Valentinian, sparing the real culprits, had the tongues of two of the leading men of Leptis, who had been drawn into the case, torn out while others were executed.[1]

Jerome, that learned Father of the Church, tells us—we remember once more his judgement, which is certainly more objective than that of most of his contemporaries—that 'Valentinian, in general, was an outstanding Emperor, in his moral tone resembling Aurelian—only some explained his excessive severity as cruelty and his economy as greed'.[2] We shall see now who the 'some' men were who brought these charges.

[1] Ammianus xxviii. 6. 20, 22–3.

[2] Hieron. *chron.* a. 2381: 'Valentinianus egregius alias imperator et Aureliano moribus similis, nisi quod severitatem eius nimiam et parcitatem quidam crudelitatem et avaritiam interpretabantur'.

IV

THE CLASH BETWEEN VALENTINIAN I AND THE GUARDIANS OF THE TRADITIONS OF ROME

VALENTINIAN was a man of great height[1] and had undergone a hard education in the army.[2] Even his enemies had to admit his personal bravery.[3] His excellence as a commander had been won in many campaigns, and he had also a special talent for the conduct of war[4] on a grand scale.

He fought with success against the Alamanni and Franks, the Quadi and the Sarmatians, and, at the same time, endeavoured to build up the system of defences along the banks of the Rhine and Danube into an impregnable fortress. Following a great strategic plan, on a scale unknown before, he protected them, partly by forts of various sizes, thrust more or less deeply into the enemy's country, while on the main line he erected forts, with block foundations and extraordinarily strong walls, and, amidst and behind them, all manner of defensive works. He set out to carry out this plan as soon as he had ascended the throne,[5] and traces of his arrangements are soon to be seen.[6] He kept steadily at work on the realization of this grandiose scheme till the day of his death.[7] He took part with admirable expertness in the drafting of the plans and often directed the carrying out of them in person.[8] At the same time

[1] Ammianus xxx. 9. 6; *Epit. de Caes.* 45. 5; Theodoret *H.E.* iv. 6. 1, &c.

[2] Ammianus xxvii. 6. 1, xxx. 7. 11; Symm. *or.* I. 4, 7.

[3] The best concrete example is given in Ammianus xxvii. 10. 10–11. O. Seeck, *Gesch. d. Unt. d. ant. Welt.* v. 12, 25, and 34, puts the facts in an unfavourable light. His false construction is justly named 'malicious' by W. Heering, op. cit. 29, 38–55. Cf. also A. Nagl, *RE.* vii A. 2203.

[4] Ammianus xxx. 7. 11 and 9. 1 and 4.

[5] When he spent half a year at the beginning of his reign on the journey from Constantinople to Milan, he was not 'loitering' (as Seeck puts it, op. cit. v. 12) but was certainly investigating with care the conditions on the military frontier of Illyricum (for his itinerary see Seeck, op. cit. 426 ff.).

[6] *Cod. Theod.* xv. 1. 13 (A.D. 364, 19 June).

[7] See Note 18, p. 133.

[8] Symm. *or.* ii. 18. 28 (1 January A.D. 370); Ammianus xxviii. 2. 1 ff.

he was busy in building up a fund out of which city walls everywhere could be put in good repair,[1] and he also arranged for the rebuilding of the much neglected complex of roads.[2]

To develop to the utmost possible perfection the system of frontier defence and fortification[3] and to suppress the movements of the peoples on the frontiers[4] was the main concern that ruled his whole being. He has only to hear that the barbarians are in motion to forget all else.[5] He is the true Roman *imperator*, conscious of his first duty, the fight against barbarism.[6] When Procopius revolted against the brother whom Valentinian had raised to the throne in the East, and when the power of Valens seemed about to collapse, Valentinian still did not move against the usurper and explained his conduct by saying that Procopius was the enemy of him and of his brother alone, while the movements of the Alamanni in south Germany constituted a threat to the whole of the Roman world.[7]

This habit of keeping the whole Empire in view is characteristic of Valentinian; it was not to be quelled or thwarted by any interests of person, family, or class. E. Schwartz, the distinguished Church historian, writes:[8] 'In the third century, the Emperors no longer came from the Roman-Italian nation, but from a motley conglomeration of officials and officers, whose only nationality was the imperial service.' In another place I

[1] A. Schulten, *Jahreshefte d. Österr. Arch. Inst.* ix, 1906, 56 ff.

[2] Ibid. 59, n. 67 (the evidence of inscriptions is collected here).

[3] Ammianus xxix. 6. 2: 'Valentinianus enim studio muniendorum limitum glorioso quidem sed nimio, ab ipso principatus initio flagrans'. The *nimio* certainly refers to a point that Ammianus explains in another passage: it is a pity to irritate the barbarians by erecting forts in their territory, because after all it is their own. He forgets that these were no innocent lambs, but peoples who grasped every conceivable opportunity of plundering the provinces; with them such restraint as he is thinking of would be quite out of place.

[4] Ibid. 4. 1: 'sollertiae vero circa rem publicam usquam digredientis nemo eum vel obtrectator pervicax incusabit, illud contemplans, quod maius pretium operae foret in coercendis verius limite barbaris quam pellendis'.   [5] Ibid. xxx. 8. 12.

[6] Ibid. xxvii. 6. 12; even if only stated in a fictitious speech, it is characteristic.

[7] See Note 19, p. 133.

[8] E. Schwartz, *Kaiser Konstantin u. die christl. Kirche*², 1936, 4.

E

have shown[1] that this ruling class of non-Italians in late Rome was no mere medley without national or even with an international character, but that it was chosen by natural selection from the most vital reserves of man-power and that it succeeded in harmonizing its local and national associations with a new and constructive patriotism to the Empire. I have further shown that the backbone of this leading group was formed by the sons of Illyricum. Not only most of the Emperors of the second half of the third century, but also the tetrarchy of Diocletian (A.D. 285–305) and the dynasty of Constantius Chlorus and his son, Constantine, came from the Illyro-Celtic soldier-folk of the Danube–Balkan territory. Most of these men, including Valentinian himself, were Pannonians. His constructive view, embracing the whole of the *imperium Romanum*, was fed by great and glorious traditions. Another important factor is this: the centre of gravity of the Empire had, since Diocletian, been pushed eastwards; but Valentinian now regarded the West as more important than the East[2] and, therefore, entrusted the latter to the lesser care of his brother. The West, as seen by Valentinian, did not mean Italy alone, but, with it, Celtic, Illyrian, and Thracian Europe; his eyes were not turned inwards, to the relatively tranquil motherland and Rome, but to the frontier where the real danger lay.

Valentinian, then, up to his accession, had been bound by every tie to the soldier class, and, throughout his reign, the disturbances and damage caused by the barbarians, who menaced him from every quarter, remained his supreme anxiety.

'In this time', says Ammianus, in his grim, emotional style, 'the trumpets of the army blew the alarm over practically the whole Empire. The wildest peoples broke in and fell upon the frontier districts near them. The Alamanni ravaged the Gallic lands and also Raetia, the Sarmatians and Quadi Pannonia; the Picts, Scots, Saxons, and Attacotti cruelly vexed Britain and gave her no peace; the Austorians and other Moorish tribes plundered Africa even more savagely than was their wont,

---

[1] *25. Jahre röm.-germ. Kommission*, 1929, 11 ff.; *C.A.H.* xii, 1939, 200 ff.
[2] This has already been observed by H. Richter, *Das weström. Reich.* 1865, 243, and further emphasized by E. Kornemann, 'Die roem. Kaiserzeit' (Gercke–Norden, *Einleitung in die Alt. Wiss.* iii¹, 1911, 231); W. Heering, op. cit. 22.

and Thrace, too, was harried by Gothic marauders. The Persian king stretched out his hand towards Armenia and made speed, with all his power, to subject it anew to his rule.'[1]

'Birds of a feather flock together.' The military and imperial schemes of Valentinian were, of course, shared by those whom he took to assist him in administering the Empire, of whom we have gained some general knowledge. We have also seen how this way of thought and its representatives had largely ousted the old aristocracy from the chief positions in administration. This process vexed the Roman notables, and their vexation is sharply mirrored in the narrative of Ammianus.[2] 'And, as we have occasion to express our opinion freely, we say openly that this Emperor was the first to aggrandize the soldiers by raising them in rank and property to the detriment of the common weal. . . . Why, now, in their arrogance they imagine that the fate of every man without distinction hangs on their nod!'[3]

A whole world separated Valentinian from the ideas of the Senate, and it is not surprising that the two came into conflict.[4] The aristocracy failed to understand the intentions of Valentinian and interpreted them as a slur on themselves; they saw in them nothing but the hatred of the proletarian for all who were better dressed, wealthy, and noble.[5] On the other hand, we can readily conceive how repugnant these senators, now mostly grown effeminate, and languishing in the glories of the past, were to a soldier Emperor, who had grown up amid fierce

[1] Ammianus xxvi. 4. 5–6: 'hoc tempore, velut per universum orbem Romanum bellicum canentibus bucinis, excitae gentes saevissimae, limites sibi proximos persultabant. Gallias Raetiasque simul Alamanni populabantur; Sarmatae Pannonias et Quadi; Picti Saxonesque et Scotti et Attacotti Britannos aerumnis vexavere continuis; Austoriani Mauricaeque aliae gentes Africam solito acrius incursabant; Thracias et [. . .] diripiebant praedatorii globi Gothorum. Persarum rex Armeniis manus iniectabat eos in suam dicionem ex integro vocare vi nimia properans . . . .'

[2] W. Ensslin, *Zur Geschichtsschreibung u. Weltanschauung des Ammianus Marcellinus*, 1923, 28.

[3] See Note 20, p. 134.

[4] The subject is dealt with in brief by O. Seeck, *Gesch. d. Unt. d. ant. Welt.* v. 15 ff.; E. Stein, *Gesch. d. spätrömischen Reiches*, i, 1928, 274; W. Ensslin, *Zur Geschichtsschreibung u. Weltanschauung d. A. M.*, 1923, 28 ff. There is not much new in L. A. A. Jouai, *De magistraat Ausonius*, 1938, 86 ff.

[5] See Note 21, p. 134.

and bloody battles and who was for ever waging war against barbarism. We have only to read the intimate letters (and other documents) of Symmachus that survive in their hundreds—Symmachus, one of the most distinguished representatives of the Roman aristocracy, who was active at the court of Valentinian—to realize how when, on a solemn occasion, he greets the Emperor with a set-piece of oratory, he has something to say about the barbarian dragon which the Emperor has been treading under foot, in general he is only concerned with it when it threatens his direct and vital interests. The fate of his 'country', of which he is so fond of talking, means to him only the fate of the *urbs*, the immunity of the property of the noble landowners, the privileges of his class. Whilst the waves of the wanderings of the peoples beat on the frontiers, these great lords sought refreshment in their palatial villas in the neighbourhood of Baiae, erected new buildings, interested themselves in science, art, ethics, or beauty, without suffering a pang for the sorrows of the frontier provinces or for the countless miseries of an Empire that embraced the whole world.

The Pannonian Emperor, puritanical, strict of life, sober and hard as he was, must have despised the average senator far more than did Ammianus Marcellinus; and yet Ammianus himself, for all the sympathy that he felt for them in many points, has but a comfortless picture of them to draw.[1] They appeal arrogantly to their descent, he tells us, and to the ancestors of their family, and, as superior beings, they despise the plain man. But, if they have anything to fear from a court dignitary of lower rank, they cringe in the dust before him. Their greedy selfishness, their intrigues to gain legacies excite the disgust of Ammianus. They are brutal in their dealings with their servants. They are lazy and effeminate. When they travel to their estates or, with help from others, kill a wild beast with the spear, they fancy that they have done something heroic. In splendid robes, surrounded by an army of servants, they appear in their equipages in the streets of Rome, with their prinked-up ladies, pushing ordinary foot-passengers into the gutter. Or again, they waste their time in the company of ladies

[1] Ammianus xxviii. 4. 6 ff. and in other places, in the form of casual remarks.

of easy virtue in the public baths. Their charioteers and their horses, their pretty damsels are to them the most important things in the world. At home they are surrounded by flatterers and gossips who praise the rich splendour of their palaces or the choice of dainties at their luxurious banquets. Their favourite reading is furnished by short historical biographies, seasoned with piquant gossip, and by biting satires; but the storehouses of true culture, the libraries, are shunned by them like the grave. So speaks Ammianus, their partisan!

No doubt this luxury was a survival of a long period of evolution, not the particular fault of this generation; so, too, were the exclusion of senators from the great military commands, their mammoth possessions and their fabulous wealth in the midst of general misery, and their undeserved privileges before the law in criminal cases. All that was really modern was their arbitrary oppression of the small man. We must admit, too, that the temper of the new men (*novi homines*) who were rising in their midst was much like their own, and that the new social order, which had already begun to take shape against them in the third century, deliberately chose to leave them at the head of society. Men could not help regarding as natural the position which the nobles, as victors, enjoyed as their right—as natural as the heavy and tragic sufferings of the slave masses. If *we* can only regard these scandalous privileges as a cancerous growth in their influence on society, Valentinian must have judged likewise; only, he was bound, as we are not, by the fact that the ruling position or, at least, the prestige of the senatorial class really had its sanction in the public morality of Rome, which essentially rested on the 'customs of our ancestors'. Even Constantine, that rash innovator, lacking any personal feeling for the past, was forced to make terms with it.

Ever since the Emperors had ceased to reside in Rome, preferring to build their palaces in the great centres of communications and administration behind the army fronts, it had been the custom for them to visit the city of their ancestors[1] at least at the beginning of the reign or at the turn of the fifth or tenth year. Valentinian neglected this obligation; and yet, at the

[1] Cf. my *The Conversion of Constantine and Pagan Rome*, 1948, 93 ff.

This does not, of course, imply that the Emperor may not in such cases have taken on himself to judge just as severely as in the cases of culprits of lower rank; and it is not out of the question that these edicts, of the first years of the reign, may have been the prelude to the actions against senators which, a few years later, produced such serious tensions.

That criminal proceedings against senators were being conducted with increased severity—even if only on a small scale—may be observed at the very beginning of the reign. Julian, in A.D. 362, is still defending 'the rights of the senators and the reputation of the class to which we belong' and prescribing that senators, under criminal prosecution, must not be held in prison; whereas Valentinian, in A.D. 365, withdraws this privilege.[1] There are indications, too, that the two imperial brothers tried to make a further improvement in the condition of the small tenants on the estates of the great landowners,[2] and also to put an end to the practice—that was then becoming so terribly common—for the small-holder, in order to escape the load of taxation, to renounce his possessions in favour of an owner of *latifundia* in the neighbourhood, who would protect him from being plagued by the creatures of the State.[3] But the defence of the small-holder, the *colonus*,[4] was bound to fail in the long run; and so, too, was the attempt to stop small-holdings from

comperto eam formam statuere possimus, quam modus facti contemplatione dictaverit. dat. VIII. id. Oct. Remis, Gratiano et Dagalaifo conss.' Cf. Mommsen, *Strafrecht*, 285.

[1] *Cod. Theod.* ix. 2. 2: 'quisquis fuerit, quem crimen pulsat, quem negotium tangit, comprehensum eum iudex sub custodia constituat atque ita vel causae meritum vel personae qualitatem ad nos referat, vel, si longius fuerimus, ad inlustres viros praefectos praetorio, sive ad magistros militum, si militaris fuerit persona, ne sub specie vel verae vel ementitae dignitatis facinora dilabantur. dabimus enim formam, quam unusquisque iudex sequetur in eo, qui reus fuerit inventus. interim ille, qui in suspicionem venerit negotii criminalis, cuiuscumque honoris esse dicatur, conprehensus ex officio non recedat.'

[2] A. Nagl, *RE.* vii A. 2192, has already rightly put this under the heading of 'clash with the Senate'.

[3] *Cod. Theod.* xi. 24. 1 ff. The law comes from Valens, but he was never anything but the executor of his brother's wishes. Cf. E. Stein, op. cit. i. 278 ff.

[4] *Cod. Theod.* xi. 1. 14 and E. Stein, op. cit., on the passage; this, too, is an Edict of Valens, but is to be judged on the same lines as the other.

being swallowed up in the attempt to secure protection (*patro-cinium*).

In any case, the new institution of the *defensores plebis*,[1] which was organized by Valentinian first in Illyricum, as it seems, and then extended to the whole of his Empire, was a gallant effort to protect the humble against the mighty land-owners. The Emperor will guarantee the poor peasant a legal defence without any fee or expense, and thus get rid of the necessity of calling in the aid of the owners of the neighbouring big estates whose protection meant the loss of freedom and property. Though Valentinian uses some polite phrases in ex-plaining to the Senate that the cases of their members in the provinces will still be dealt with in the future by the normal authorities,[2] he is very explicit on the point that his special care for the *innocens et quieta rusticitas*[3] is intended *contra potentium iniurias*.[4] In this endeavour he could not rely upon the Senate, nor upon the members of the city councils, nor upon the officials of the prefects and governors, but only on men who had won distinction in the provincial administration or in the service of his Court.[5] This is the same class of men from which all the confidants of this sovereign were chosen in his struggle with the senatorial oligarchy, championing the rights of the peasants against their oppressors.

The law of Valentinian about precedence,[6] again, points to the same direction. It is not the isolated case that it once was supposed to be; it was just one step forward in a long develop-ment. By these enactments Valentinian let the generals (*magi-stri militum*) attain the rank of *praefecti praetorio*,[7] whereas till then it had been the prefects who headed the official gradation;

---

[1] *Cod. Theod.* i. 29. 1 ff. Cf. A. Hoepffner, 'Un aspect de la lutte de Valen-tinien Ier contre le Sénat, la création du defensor plebis' (*Revue hist.* clxxxii, 1938, 225 ff.); A. Piganiol, op. cit. 185 f. and n. 92.

[2] 'hoc fieri dignitas non patitur senatoris. . . . ordinaria sine dubio rectoris habeatur auctoritas, quae meliore in bonos condicione retinetur', *Cod. Theod.* i. 29. 5.   [3] Ibid.   [4] Ibid. 1.

[5] 'aliquos idoneis moribus . . . tua sinceritas ad hoc eligere curet officium, qui aut provinciis praefuerunt aut forensium stipendiorum egere militiam aut inter agentes in rebus palatinosque meruerunt'. *Cod. Theod.*, loc. cit.

[6] Seeck, *Gesch. d. Unt. d. ant. Welt*, v. 16.

[7] *Cod. Theod.* vi. 7. 1.

he also exalted the rank of the *comites rei militaris* to the side of the *vicarii*.[1] This put an end to the predominance of the civil officials over the military. But the conditions that inspired this move, as we have seen, go very far back in history. The revolution of the third century, which deprived the Senate of the command over the army corps, had, in actual fact, raised the career of the professional soldier over that of the senator. The commander of the cavalry under Gallienus was, next to the Emperor, the most powerful man in the Empire.[2] Even more vital was it that the throne was reached by a series of military men who had begun service as private soldiers, and that the path that led to the throne was barred to the senators. And yet, for all that, when Constantine gave final shape to the many-terraced pyramid of the hierarchy of the late Roman State, it was the rank of senator that came out on the top; that was the fortress which the holders of the new posts at Court and the newfangled ranks in the army held under continual siege[3] until, finally, first the civil, and then the military, dignitaries attained the rank of senator and even outsoared it, by the creation of new and growingly impressive titles and ranks. Thus the band of imperial functionaries, superior in actual strength, gradually overtook the senatorial class, that soared aloft on its tradition, in this sphere of external privileges as well. It is certainly the case—and, from this point of view, no accident—that it was Valentinian who placed his generals at the head of the civil career.[4]

Still less can we ascribe it to chance that our Emperor made a great advance along the path that transformed the senatorial class from a closed social group to a closed social stratum, in which the mass of courtiers of lower origin, now raised to the Senate, reduced the aristocracy, with its pride of ancestry, to a minority. Not only did the *vicarii*, who included some senators, gain the title of *clarissimus*, but also the senior holders of offices at Court on their retirement from service—even in cases where they were descended from freedmen.[5] Valentinian's in-

---

[1] *Cod. Theod.* vi. 14. 1.   [2] A. Alföldi, *C.A.H.* xii. 217.
[3] Cf. Id., *The Conversion of Constantine and Pagan Rome*, 1948, 110 ff.
[4] Cf. also W. Ensslin, *Klio*, xxiii, 1929, 306 ff., xxiv. 1930, 102 ff. and 467 ff.
[5] *Cod. Theod.* vi. 9. 1, 22. 4; 35. 7; *Cod. Iust.* xii. 1. 9; O. Hirschfeld,

tention certainly was, not only to exalt the rank of the personnel of the Court, but also to dissolve the senators, privileged by birth, in the masses of those who won their dignity through the imperial service. What was involved was a gradual transformation of the Senate already prepared by earlier Emperors, raising its numbers to 2,000—in all probability—, in Rome as well as in Constantinople.

It would be a grave mistake to suppose that the antipathy of Valentinian to the Senate concerned Rome as a whole. The Emperor, like Constantine before him,[2] tried to revive the order of knights, which had fallen into the shadows of oblivion, in a new scope, limited to Rome,[3] by investing its members with important privileges.

An important event in the cultural life of the Eternal City was that new order of studies which gave a new basis to the training that qualified for the highest posts and reasserted the central position of Rome in this sphere.[4] Valentinian also showed the greatest goodwill to Rome, as to other places,[5] in his care for the lower orders of society.

Contemporaries are already found comparing Valentinian,

Kleine Schriften, 1913, 665, 668 f.; O. Seeck, *Reg.* 242 (5 July A.D. 372), the same, *Gesch. d. Unt. d. ant. Welt*, ii². 67, 507; A. Grosse, *Röm. Militärgeschichte*, 1920, 154 ff.; E. Stein, op. cit. i. 274.

[1] Ausonius, *prof.* I. 9 f.: 'iuvenes bis mille senatui adiecit numero purpureisque togis'; Themistius, *or.* 34. 13 (p. 456 Dind.): τὸν κατάλογον τῶν ὁμογενῶν ἀντὶ μόλις τριακοσίων ἐπλήρουν εἰς δισχιλίους. He succeeded, then, during his proconsulate in A.D. 358–9 in raising the Senate of Constantinople from 300 to 2,000 members (cf. Seeck, *Die Briefe d. Lib.* 298 ff.).

[2] A. Alföldi, *Journ. Rom. Stud.* xxxvii, 1947, 10 ff.

[3] *Cod. Theod.* vi. 37. I = *Cod. Iust.* xii. 31. I (31 October A.D. 364): 'impp. Val(entini)anus et Valens A.A. ad Mamertinum praefectum praetorio. equites Romani, quos secundi gradus in urbe omnium optinere volumus dignitatem, ex indigenis Romanis et civibus eligantur, vel his peregrinis, quos corporatis non oportet adnecti. et quia vacuos huiusmodi viros esse privilegiis non oportet, corporalium eos iniuriarum et prosecutionum formido non vexet, ab indictionibus quoque, quae senatorium ordinem manent habebuntur immunes. dat. prid. Kal. Nov. Philippopoli divo Ioviano et Varroniano conss.'

[4] *Cod. Theod.* xiv. 9. I. cf. H. L. Marrou, *Histoire de l'éducation dans l'antiquité*, 1948, 406 ff.

[5] Cf., for example, H. Schiller, *Gesch. d. r. Kaiserzeit*, ii, 1887, 368 ff.;

the brave, strict, and harsh, whose main concern was the defence of the provinces, with a predecessor of similar character, Aurelian.[1] The comparison also fits, in so far as both came into conflict with the Senate and both took the most energetic measures to provide for the material welfare of the people—for their supply of food, in the first place. In the very first months of his reign, when he came from the East to Italy, Valentinian begins the long series of ordinances which served to ameliorate the lot of the *plebs urbana.*

Above all, Valentinian made a complete reform in the supply of bread to the citizens of Rome. Whereas hitherto they had received a certain amount of bread of the worst quality (*panis sordidus*) at a low price, they now had distributed to them two thirds of the same quantity of the finest bread (*bucellus mundus*)—here again Valentinian was following the procedure of Aurelian. This great benefit was designed, directly and uniquely, for the successors in law of the proud old *populus Romanus*; but provision was also made for the poorer residue of the population of the city through local distributing centres of cheap bread.[2] For the bread that was to be delivered for payment Valentinian allotted to the bakers 200,000 modii of wheat at prices below the market—that had been the amount since the time of Caesar—and he gave the strictest injunctions that the quality was to be above reproach,[3] in order that the honoured *plebs* might get good bread. He issued all manner of edicts to prevent the vile corruption of the age from frustrating his arrangements: the shippers, who deliver the grain, must supply certificates to show that the grain that they have taken over is sound and not spoiled and, on the arrival of the ships in Portus, the harbour of Rome,[4] the authorities have to check them: the hungry personnel of the Chancellory are kept away from the arrangements for supply and from criminal exchange of the bread that was delivered daily to the distributing centres

O. Seeck, *Gesch. d. Unt. d. ant. Welt,* v. 421; E. Stein, *Gesch. d. spätröm. Reiches,* i. 277 ff.

[1] Ammianus xxx. 8. 8; Hieron. *chron.* a. 2381.
[2] See Note 23, p. 135 and the new inscription, *CRA* i, 1949, 16 ff.; cf. also B. Kübler, *RE,* 18. 2. 606 ff.   [3] *Cod. Theod.* xiv. 15. 1 (1 July A.D. 364).
[4] Ibid. 2 (14 June A.D. 366).

(*panis gradilis*),[1] and others too[2] were held off. Valentinian also saw to it that the old stocks in the corn-magazines should be used up first and that they should only be mixed with new grain when the old was spoilt; he further enacted that reliable controllers should supervise the proceedings;[3] he had the great official granaries in Rome and Portus put into good repair, and, when private individuals presumed to occupy them, he had them evicted.[4] In a word, he was attentive to the smallest details: they were his most intimate concern. The supreme administration of the corn-supply was also reorganized by him.[5]

Further, Valentinian saw to it that the shippers should arrange for the smooth transport of the African grain from overseas. These shippers were always endeavouring, by all possible means, to escape the intolerably severe charges laid on them; some succeeded in gaining admission to the Senate, others changed their addresses, or tried, by sale or even by free gift of their property, immobile and otherwise, to free themselves from the burdens of the compulsory guild of *navicularii*, or attempted to free the property that passed on the female side from these loads. Others, again, pretended that their transports had fallen victims to storms at sea. All these designs Valentinian, in the interests of the provisioning of the Roman people, set himself with energy to thwart.[6]

Besides all this, it was vital that the great bakeries which produced the vast masses of bread, distributed in Rome free or at low prices, should be perfect in their functioning. All to no purpose had the bakers, marked out as such by their birth, been united in a single caste, in order that they might not evade their heavy obligations. They still found means of evasion, and Valentinian, therefore, was concerned to thwart them. A baker was forbidden to hand over his property to a senator or an official (*officialis*)—for both these classes were so hard to get

[1] Ibid. 17. 2 (9 December A.D. 364).
[2] Ibid. 3 and 4 (4 April A.D. 368), and also 6 (19 March A.D. 370).
[3] Ibid. xi. 14. 1.   [4] Ibid. xv. 1. 12 (8 June A.D. 364).
[5] Ibid. i. 6. 5 (4 April A.D. 368).
[6] Ibid. xiii. 5. 11 (11 January A.D. 365), xiii. 5. 12 (14 May A.D. 369), xiii. 6. 2 (11 June A.D. 365), xiii. 6. 3 (31 July A.D. 368 or 37 oor 373?), xiii. 6. 4 (28 April A.D. 367), xiii. 6. 5 (29 September A.D. 367), xiii. 6. 6 (7 April A.D. 372), xiii. 6. 7 (3 August A.D. 375), xiii. 9. 2 (A.D. 372–5).

hold of—lest the capital on which the compulsory trade depended should vanish. The *pistor* is only allowed to make presents inside his family to such as, by reason of their birth, are directly engaged to continue the business, and only when the recipient of the gift voluntarily accepts the liability.[1] And, when a family of bakers inherits money or immobile property from whatever source, these same acquisitions are ear-marked for the purposes of the corporation even while they remain in the possession of the heir.[2] If the owner of a bakery succeeded in shaking off his obligations by securing admission to the roll of senators, he must either renounce such of his property as belonged to the business, or abdicate his new rank, unless he could put a new baker in his place.[3] He could not himself be discharged from his corporation, even if all other members of it gave their consent.[4] Nor might he enter any priestly guild.[5] The Emperor also ensured that the property on the female side should not be withdrawn from the guild of bakers.[6] The *proconsul Africae* is required, on pain of the most severe penalties, to send to the Eternal City, every five years, bakers belonging to the office subordinate to himself.[7]

Into the corporation of the *catabolenses*, who arranged for the dispatch of grain to the bakers, he admitted even freedmen, if they possessed the necessary property,[8] and, if bakers ever allowed their own enfranchised slaves a share in their property, these slaves too had to become bakers.[9] The orphan children of bakers were only set free by Valentinian from the exercise of their responsible trade till their twentieth year; even before they reached that age a representative had to be installed in their stead. These representatives were not released from baking even when the orphans attained the age prescribed.[10] Only the most senior leaders of the baking industry were allowed by Valentinian to take their discharge after a blameless activity of five years, on condition that they delivered

---

[1] *Cod. Theod.* xiv. 3. 3 (2 June A.D. 364).   [2] Ibid. 13 (13 June A.D. 369).
[3] Ibid. 4 (6 June A.D. 364).   [4] Ibid. 8 (15 January A.D. 365).
[5] Ibid. 11 (27 September A.D. 365).   [6] Ibid.14 (22 February A.D. 372).
[7] Ibid. 12 (1 December A.D. 370).
[8] Ibid. 9 (30 March A.D. 368 or 370?).
[9] Ibid. 10 (7 July A.D. 368 or 370?).   [10] Ibid. 5 (8 June A.D. 364).

to their successors the entire equipment of their business.[1] These ordinances, in part reinforcing older orders, which seem to us so cruel, were regularly followed by the successors of Valentinian to the end. The good intention seemed to justify them.

Valentinian also improved the delivery of the wine that was required for the Roman masses, by forbidding the Italian provincials engaged in delivering it from discharging their obligations in money, and, further, he guaranteed to the wine-merchants a fourth of the market price as profit, to make them the readier to co-operate in the delivery.[2] He also tried to increase the quantities of pigs raised in Lucania and Bruttium, by granting indemnities to the forced corporations engaged in the business there,[3] and to arrange for sufficient cooking-oil for the Romans.[4] The privileges of the guilds (*corporati*), which arranged for the deliveries and favours designed for the *plebs urbana*, were enhanced by Valentinian, after having been apparently[5] reduced by Julian.[6] The ships that sailed the Tiber were, without exception, forced by Valentinian into the service of the general deliveries.[7] Valentinian ensured profit to the corporations of sack- and barrel-porters by assuring to them what they had earned by private transport;[8] and he also fixed the privileges and incomes of the charcoal-burners and suppliers of materials for building.[9] He fought against the decline that was visible in the compulsory fire-brigade of the city (*centonarii*).[10] He was also concerned to prevent the authorities in the city, in those days of misery, from putting up new buildings, requiring them instead to repair the decayed splendours

[1] Ibid. 7 (8 October A.D. 367).

[2] Ibid. xi. 2. 1 (12 August A.D. 365), ibid. 2 (23 October A.D. 365?): cf. xiv. 6. 3 and xiv. 4. 4.

[3] Ibid. xiv. 4. 4 (8 October A.D. 367?), with the commentary of Gothofredus.

[4] Cf. *Cambridge Mediaeval History*, i. 551 ff. (P. Vinogradoff).

[5] See the commentary of Gothofredus on the law in *Cod. Theod.* xiii. 5. 10.

[6] Ibid. xiv. 2. 1 (1 June A.D. 364).

[7] Ibid. 21. 1 (8 October A.D. 364).   [8] Ibid. 22. 1 (8 June A.D. 364).

[9] Ibid. 6. 2 (8 June A.D. 362), ibid. 3 (6 August A.D. 365): 'statum urbis aeternae reformare cupientes ac providere publicorum moenium dignitati iubemus', &c.   [10] Ibid. 8. 2 (28 January A.D. 369).

of the past.[1] Further, he provided for the wood needed to heat the great public baths of Rome and for its delivery.[2] How brilliant was his performance in this sphere is revealed by the circumstance that, in the code of Theodosius II, most of the edicts relating to these matters are derived from him.[3] But it is interesting to observe how, now and then, antagonism to the senatorial class can be seen in these edicts. After reorganizing the distribution of bread in A.D. 369[4] and allowing others besides the *cives Romani* to profit by it, he supplemented his edicts by others that dealt most severely with abuses committed by dependants and servants of the senators in connexion with the distribution of bread, and in the case of complicity on the part of the master, punished him by the confiscation of his property.[5]

The same tendency is revealed in the text of another Edict of Valentinian of A.D. 368, in which he appointed, with an official salary, a doctor to each of the fourteen districts of the old capital and enjoined on these *archiatri* that, 'realizing that their daily bread came to them from the property of the (Roman) people, they should, as was right, stand at the disposal of the poor and not simply serve the rich.'[6] Both enactments are dated to the period of Maximinus' office in Rome and both bear the stamp of his violent hatred rather than of the bitter rectitude of Valentinian.

Again, the notable activities of Valentinian in building in Rome served, in the first place, the good and the interests of the people.[7] Above all, the building of at least two (or, it may be, three) bridges over the Tiber represents a mighty achievement.[8] A forum built (or repaired?) by the two imperial brothers was

---

[1] *Cod. Theod.* xv. 1. 11 (25 May A.D. 364).

[2] Ibid. xiii. 5. 10 (8 March? A.D. 364), ibid. 13 (2 December A.D. 369), xiv. 5. 1 (3 April A.D. 368 or 370).

[3] Cf. also H. Schiller, op. cit. ii, 1887, 369 ff.

[4] *Cod. Theod.* xiv. 17. 5.

[5] See Note 24, p. 135.

[6] 'qui scientes annonaria sibi commoda a populi commodis ministrari, honeste obsequi tenuioribus malint, quam turpiter servire divitibus': *Cod. Theod.* xiii. 3. 8 (30 January A.D. 368–70).

[7] For further detail see A. Nagl, *RE.* vii A. 2194 ff. Cf. also Platner–Ashby, *A Topogr. Dict. of Anc. Rome*, 1929, 229, 399, 420, 421.

[8] Cf. Mommsen, *Ges. Schriften*, vii. 391.

dedicated by them to 'their Roman people'.[1] The rebuilding of the Forum of Livia[2] was a measure designed to serve the common weal, as were the works of restoration on the aqueducts.[3] Valentinian's fatherly care for the people of Rome was such that, more than a century later, his name stood first, beside that of Trajan, in the eyes of the *plebs urbana*.[4]

Such was the atmosphere in which the clash developed between the Pannonian soldier who had ascended the throne and the senatorial circles, when Valentinian, with an iron hand, tried to interfere with the sinful practices of the private life of the Roman aristocracy. Looked at in the mass it is a set of legal cases, bloody and exasperating, which were, for the most part, tried under the rule of Maximinus and his successors of similar disposition. There were two main themes—two and only two. The material consisted first of magic, second of adultery; magic used to seduce women or secure the victory of a partisan driver in the circus—sometimes combined with attempts on the life of the Emperor: one and all were capital charges, as, too, was the mere copying of a book containing magical prescriptions. The harsh spirit of the age punished even adultery, whether in man or woman, with the death sentence.

Of these cases Ammianus supplies most detailed and incredibly one-sided reports.[5] It will be well worth our while to illustrate, with some fullness, the distortions of truth of which he is guilty, because they show up so sharply the passions and other weaknesses characteristic of the party that suffered, the aristocracy, while we learn in detail—all too much detail—to know the weaknesses of the winning side, the Pannonians. When we have got to know the faults of the two parties that stood confronted with so little mutual understanding, we shall also have a better insight into their virtues.

[1] 'populo romano suo': *C.I.L.* vi. 1177 = Dessau 776; *Année epigr.* 1934, no. 151.　　　[2] *C.I.L.* vi. 1178.　　　[3] Ibid. 3866.

[4] *Exc. Vales.* 60.

[5] Ammianus xxviii. 1. 1 ff.; W. Ensslin, *Zur Geschichtsschreibung u. Weltanschauung des Amm. Marc.* 1923, 28 ff., has rightly judged the attitude of Ammianus and has effectively brought out the passages that are characteristic of his prejudice. Others too had an inkling that our author is not quite correct; cf. Ch. Lécrivain, *Le Sénat romain depuis Dioclétien*, 1888, 136.

The picture that Ammianus draws of these cases of magic is shaped and coloured to make exciting reading. It is like those innumerable products of art that deliberately sacrifice the factual rendering of their theme to dramatic effects. There can be no possible doubt that Ammianus, in his description, was decisively influenced by his great model, Tacitus, in whose *Annals* the reign of Tiberius is depicted as a fearful tyranny on the ground of just such charges of high treason and similar offences against that Roman aristocracy that sighed for the free republic. If Ammianus' classical model himself exaggerated and darkened the colours, in Ammianus with even greater lack of justice the light colours are laid on for the aristocrats and the dark for the Government. In Ammianus the main theme of Tacitus ('igitur verso civitatis statu nihil usquam prisci et integri moris', *Ann.* i. 4) is taken over and reinforced: the Republic is a wreck, morality is lost; but the mainstay of the Republic, the Senate, still stands; the justice that can awaken the State to new life is in its possession; to it every man who has a serious moral standpoint, the *vir bonus*, looks, while he despises the means used to suppress it, the *dominatio*. Further, we can discover in Ammianus, in his vivid and impressive narrative, still more sources for his distortion of the facts. One is the historical work which served him as the basis of his narrative, i.e. the *Annals* of Nicomachus Flavianus, who energetically represented the interests of the great senatorial families. The other is the expression of Ammianus' own personal feelings, in which insults to himself play a large part; and finally, he was not only a partisan of the Roman nobles but was also impregnated with the ideas of classical Greece on virtue and culture—conflicting with the ideals of the Pannonian courtiers.

We shall demonstrate later that the spirit of the historians of the age was entirely senatorial, and that the production of historical works lay wholly in the hands of senators and their adherents.[1] Nor must we forget that it was the only form of

---

[1] H. Peter, *Die geschichtliche Literatur über die Kaiserzeit bis Theodosius I.*, vol. 2, 1897, 1 ff. The imputation of *inmanes et barbari mores* was already used by Cicero (*in Vatin.* 6. 14) as a weapon of rhetorical invective.

publicity available. We shall also see how the Senate later overthrew its Pannonian adversaries and their allies. That is the reason why, in the work of Nicomachus, the depreciation of the fallen enemy is at the same time an attempt to find moral justification for the conduct of his own side. The lack of any moderation in invective, to which we shall also come back later, reflects the spirit of the age, that abstract method of thought that tries to claim a hundred-per-cent. validity for all its assertions. In the bitter quarrels of Church literature we are so accustomed to finding men representing their own party as pure angels and their enemies as devils incarnate, that the modern Church historian cannot be troubled to run down all such distortions of facts in detail, but tacitly makes his corrections. Profane literature, on the other hand, has not yet learned to reduce such exaggerations to their proper scale, though in Ammianus the tendency is clear enough. In describing certain episodes in the terrorism of Maximinus his style rises to the nerve-racking horror of a detective novel.

When we study the text of the great historian of late Rome with closer care we are astounded by the wild prejudice with which he treats the Pannonians. We can hear the very cry of the arrogant oligarchs in his discussion of Maximinus, the chief scapegoat. How dare a man like him, born at the world's end, of barbarian origin, undeservedly climb from obscurity to high rank?[1] How dare he pronounce sentence on the most distinguished descendants of old Rome?[2] How dare he contend with the cream of the high nobility and with Petronius Probus?[3] No wonder that, when this vile, low-born creature (*despicatissimae sortis*) became prefect of Gaul, the twigs of the broom that was to sweep out the senate-house blossomed. One could easily foresee that the scum of the population was rising above the aristocracy.[4]

---

[1] Ammianus xxviii. 1. 5.
[2] Cf. W. Ensslin, op. cit., who emphasizes also the next points that I shall make in the text.
[3] Ammianus xxviii. 1. 31: 'viri summatum omnium maximi'.
[4] Ibid. 1. 42: 'in id tempus aut non multo prius scopae florere sunt visae, quibus nobilitatis curia mundabatur. idque portendebat, extollendos quosdam despicatissimae sortis ad gradus potestatum excelsos'.

Ammianus makes no secret of the fact that he is only interested in what happens to the members of the noble families and is not concerned to write of the fortunes of all sorts of 'dirty folk'.[1] He only records the names of ordinary persons when they are involved in some scandal that affects the Senate—and then only if he has to. Otherwise, he will, at most, mention[2] the existence of such 'inferiors' (*humiles*), whereas, in the case of the high nobility, he never omits to record their origin and their ancestors.[3] It leaves him quite cold that the examination of wretched slaves should take place under torture, but he is furious when a confession, extorted on the rack from 'a scrap of humanity sunk in endless filth', might actually be used against his noble master.[4] But if, in a case of high treason, investigation under torture was employed against senators, then it is an inhuman (imperial) edict, surpassing in its rude brutality all known precedents.[5] He is beside himself with rage that the Government is now venturing 'in unheard-of and forbidden ways'[6] to torment those who, by the right of their ancestry, by the expressed will of the deified Emperors had been released from bloody examination.[7] Yet he himself admits elsewhere that,[8] in the spirit of the *leges Corneliae*, the fact that the crime under investigation was high treason invalidated that class privilege.[9] It is difficult to credit the boundless hatred that

[1] Ammianus xxviii. 1. 15: 'non omnia narratu sunt digna, quae per squalidas transiere personas'.   [2] Ibid. 1. 15.

[3] Ibid. 1. 17: 'Hymettii praeclarae indolis viri'; 28: 'feminae . . . originis altae'; 30: 'Aginatium . . . iam inde a priscis maioribus nobilem'; 38: 'ortu nobiles' (the word often recurs); 48: 'ambo ex coetu amplissimo'; 52: 'homo patriciae stirpis'; 54: 'senator perspicui generis'.

[4] Ibid. 1. 55: '. . . mancipia squalore diuturno marcentia, in domini caput ad usque ultimum lacerabat exitium'.

[5] Ibid. 1. 25: 'crudele praeceptum supergressum omnia diritatis exempla'.

[6] Ibid. 1. 24: 'inusitato et inlicito more'.

[7] Ibid. 1. 11: '(Valentinianus) omnes quos iuris prisci iustitia, divorumque arbitria, quaestionibus exemere cruentis, si postulasset negotium, statuit tormentis adfligi'.

[8] Ibid. xix. 12. 1 ff.

[9] Cf. F. G. A. Wasserschleben, *De quaestionum per tormenta apud Romanos historia*, 1837, 48 ff.; Mommsen, *Strafrecht*, 405 ff.; A. Ehrhardt, *RE.* vi A. 1782 ff.

raged in the soul of a writer, generally so moderate, sober, and far-sighted. When Maximinus discovered the countless offences of the former *magister officiorum*, Remigius, who, as an accomplice, had cloaked the hair-raising villainies of the scandalous Count Romanus, Ammianus cannot see the hand of avenging justice, but abuses the Pannonian *praefectus praetorio* in these words: 'raging, as was his wont, like a deadly pestilence, he tried to do him all the harm in his power'.[1]

Whilst Ammianus recounts with horror the tormenting of senators, he positively revels in describing the agonizing death by fire of one of the judges, a *vicarius urbis*.[2] Although he has only a vague rumour to go on,[3] he reports that Maximinus kept at his side a Sardinian who, in order to be enabled to prophesy, performed such sacrifices with magic rites as are forbidden under the death penalty; but, later, Maximinus had him put out of the way.[4]

In the eyes of Ammianus, Maximinus is a wild beast that crawls out of its cage in the amphitheatre to spend its innate fury on its victims.[5] His friend from Pannonia, Leo, the *magister officiorum*, is a blood-thirsty Pannonian brigand who defiles graves.[6] Another of his friends, Festus, the *magister memoriae*

---

[1] Ibid. xxx. 2. 11: 'ut solebat dirae luis ritu grassari per omnia, laedere modis quibus poterat adfectabat'.

[2] Ibid. xxviii. 1. 57: 'sed vigilarunt ultimae dirae caesorum. . . . Doryforianum . . . princeps exinde rapuit . . . (et) . . . per cruciatus oppressit immensos'. Symmachus greets this execution with equal satisfaction: 'adhibuisti' (Gratiane) 'severitatem, qualem reliqui principes maiestati tantum negotiis exhibebant'.

[3] Ibid. 1. 7: 'ut circumtulit rumor'.

[4] He also puts down to the discredit of Maximinus a crime characteristic of the weakness of late Rome, the execution of the king of the Quadi by Marcellinus, the son of Maximinus, no doubt on the order of the Emperor (xxix. 6. 3 ff., xxx. 5. 3): he does not always express himself so in similar cases; cf., for example, the description of the conduct of Julian. Cf. C. Patsch, *Beitr.* iv. 12, and my comments in *Daci e Romani in Transilvania*, 1940, 30.

[5] Ammianus xxviii. 1. 10: 'Maximinus effudit genuinam ferociam, pectori crudo adfixam, (ut saepe faciunt amphitheatrales ferae) diffractis tandem solutae posticis'; cf. 38.

[6] Ibid. 1. 12: 'Leonem notarium, postea officiorum magistrum, bustuarium quendam latronem Pannonium, efflantem ferino rictu crudelitatem, etiam ipsum nihilo minus humani sanguinis avidissimum'. Cf. Cicero, *In Pisonem*, 9. 16. 19.

and proconsul of Asia, comes of an unknown family of the lowest extraction.[1] And yet all these men were not one whit worse than their contemporaries. There is the same distortion in Ammianus' account of the part played by Valentinian. In the case of high treason against Hymetius, the proconsul of Asia, Valentinian sent the appeal of the accused to the Senate to decide, and that was certainly a gesture of goodwill towards that noble order. Indeed, it may be that Valentinian was in fact furiously angry because the Senate only punished the capital offence with banishment;[2] but that does not alter the fact that he approved the verdict.

We must also see deliberate distortion when Ammianus blackens the characters of the *vicarii* who sided with the Emperor, but passes over in silence the behaviour of the governors of the city who showed as much cowardice on the occasion of the *causes célèbres* as if they had not been there. Most curious is the fact that the prefects of Rome, Bappo, Principius, and Eupraxius, who held office from (at latest) 22 August 372 to (at the earliest) 14 February 374, i.e. in the very years of those terrifying trials, are not mentioned at all in the very detailed account of Ammianus, who elsewhere devotes so much high praise to Eupraxius. That this omission is a deliberate one has already been realized by E. A. Thompson.[3] It is clear that our author suppresses the mention of those prefects to free them from the odium of those persecutions of the nobility.

He praises the other governors, one after another—Apronianus, for example, for his decent severity;[4] and yet we are astonished to discover that the conduct of which Ammianus approves is the very same sort of trial for magic, with its bloody end, for which Valentinian and his friends have been so violently abused. This honourable gentleman, who had been appointed already by Julian, had lost the sight of one eye, and, as he was absolutely convinced that his enemies had done this to him by

[1] Ammianus xxix. 2. 22: 'Festus quidam Tridentinus, ultimi sanguinis et ignoti, in nexum germanitatis a Maximino dilectus', &c. On his innocence of this reproach see A. Schulten, *Jahreshefte*, ix, 1906, 63.

[2] Ibid. xxviii. 1. 23. On the case of Hymetius cf. E. A. Thompson, op. cit. 139.

[3] Ammianus xxviii. 1. 23.

[4] Ammianus xxvi. 3. 1 ff.

magic,[1] he made furious search for these magicians. Thus, for example, he ordered the butchery of Hilarinus, the charioteer, who had wished to have his son trained as a magician, after the poor wretch had been dragged from an altar of Christ at which he had sought refuge. Our author does just mention that some people regarded this as black cruelty,[2] but he only records the opinion, without adhering to it. But he simply books the case of the senator who, like Hilarinus with his son, had his slave initiated into the mysterious hocus-pocus of the magicians, yet when he was detected procured his acquittal by bribery in order to be able to swagger about the streets of Rome, instead of being ashamed, sinner that he was, to continue to live.[3]

Of the prefecture of Olybrius, too, Ammianus writes as if in his time nothing disagreeable had happened anywhere in the world;[4] and yet it was this very Olybrius on whose proposal Maximinus was entrusted, in his stead, with the task of investigating the charges of magic.[5] And why is there no mention in Ammianus of the fact that the *nobilis aduliscens* Alypius, who was banished during the trials now discussed for a 'slight offence', was no other than the brother of the prefect Olybrius?[6] Again, in describing the activities of the *praefectus urbi*, Ampelius, Ammianus has not a word to spare for the *causes célèbres*;[7] although we hear of him elsewhere, that in the case of the charge of magic against the soothsayer, Amantius and the proconsul, Hymetius, the latter was heard by Ampelius in

[1] Ibid. xxvi. 3. 2: 'iusto quidem sed inusitato dolore haec et alia magna quaeritabat industria'.

[2] Ibid. 'unde quibusdam atrox visus est, in amphitheatrali curriculo undatim coeunte aliquotiens plebe, causas dispiciens criminum maximorum'.

[3] Ibid. 4–5. Ammianus is anxious not to get into trouble by the report of these events and suppresses the name: cf. E. A. Thompson, op. cit. 108 ff.

[4] Ammianus xxviii. 4. 1: 'exorsus ab Olybrii praefectura, tranquilla nimis et leni, qui numquam ab humanitatis statu deiectus, sollicitus erat et anxius, nequid usquam factum eius asperum inveniretur aut dictum, calumniarum acerrimus insectator, fisci lucra unde poterat circumcidens, iustorum iniustorumque distinctor, et arbiter plenus, in subiectos admodum temperatus'.

[5] Ibid. 1. 32.

[6] Ibid. 1. 16; cf. E. A. Thompson, op. cit. 104.

[7] Ammianus xxviii. 4. 31.

conjunction with Maximinus, and the facts were subsequently laid before the Emperor. Instead Ammianus gives a particularly full account of his regulations for the inns and places of amusement, as though nothing else had happened under his rule.[1]

Again, after Maximinus had left for Gaul, our historian reserves all his abuse for the *vicarii*, Ursicinus, Simplicius, and Doryphorianus, as the instigators of the persecution of the nobility, as if there had been no governors of the city there at all,[2] as already mentioned.

At the same time Ammianus writes up the persecutions of the senators into veritable tales of terror.[3] He has countless deeds of horror to recount. In Rome everyone was dreaming about awful forms of death.[4] Maximinus persecutes the aristocracy madly, he himself lies in wait for his victims and sends his creatures on their track.[5] His successor, Simplicius of Emona,[6] rivals him in these courses,—Simplicius, whose cruelty outdoes the monstrous tyrants of fabulous antiquity.[7] We can test Ammianus' exaggerations best in the case of Aginatius, who was *vicarius urbis* about A.D. 370 in the days of the *praefectus urbi* Olybrius, at the same time that Maximinus held the office of *praefectus annonae* in Rome.

Ammianus cautiously states, by way of prelude, that his account is based on a persistent rumour and naïvely adds 'for there is no proof to establish it'.[8] Shielded by this alibi, he proceeds to give free play to his imagination under the inspiration of hate.

The fact is that Aginatius was not the innocent lamb that Ammianus makes him out to be. It comes out[9] that he was vexed because the investigations into magic were not, in the absence of the *praefectus urbi*, assigned to him, the *vicarius*, but to the *praefectus annonae*. He therefore tried to excite

---

[1] Ammianus xviii. 1. 22.   [2] Ibid. 1. 43 ff.   [3] Ibid. 1. 14 and 15.
[4] Ibid. 1. 16.   [5] Ibid. 1. 36–7.   [6] Ibid. 1. 46.
[7] In the same way he exaggerates the acts of terror in the cases of magic under Valens, as we can show from his own words (xxix. 1. 25): 'Pergamius . . . multa hominum milia (!) quasi consciorum sine fine strependo fundebat'.
[8] See Note 25, p. 135.
[9] Ammianus xxviii. 1. 32–3. E. A. Thompson, op. cit. 104, came independently to conclusions similar to those sketched above.

Petronius Probus to join him in twisting the tail of Maximinus. Probus, however, refused—out of correctness or more probably, out of cowardice—to come into conflict with the dignitary who enjoyed the confidence of the Emperor and sent to him the letter of the intriguing *vicarius*.[1] Aginatius then spread the rumour that Victorinus, a confidant of Maximinus, who had just died, had been selling Maximinus' verdicts for money. He thus blackened the man's memory, though he himself harvested considerable sums out of the legacy of Victorinus. He also threatened the widow with accusations, upon which she resolved to escape under the wing of Maximinus.[2]

In his description of this conflict, with its bloody ending, we can often catch out Ammianus in serious distortions of the truth. For example, we may perhaps assume that Maximinus as *praefectus praetorio* in Gaul used his influence with the Emperor, there resident, against Aginatius; but it is quite incredible that he kept in his own hands the imperial order, giving the death sentence, because he dared not have it carried out by his friend Simplicius but selected for this purpose a special accomplice, in the person of Doryphorianus, and later appointed him in place of Simplicius as *vicarius* and delivered the letter of Valentinian into his charge. This will certainly not do; the imperial order must have been addressed to a particular man by name. And if the imperial letter[3] really contained orders for the execution of Aginatius,[4] what point is there in the whole farce of hiring Doryphorianus to do the murder, what point in Doryphorianus' having to look so long for an opportunity to destroy Aginatius?[5] If the Emperor had really given the order, the execution would have been a very simple matter. When a testimony was wrung under torture out of the slaves of Aginatius against their master,[6] Ammianus describes this as illegal 'because our gentle laws forbid the use of torture in cases of adultery'. But here he is forgetting what he has already said.

[1] Ammianus xxviii. 1. 31–3.
[2] Ibid. 1. 34–35.
[3] Ibid. 1. 52–3: 'imperiale praeceptum', 'Augustae litterae'.
[4] Ibid. 1. 51: 'ut rescriberetur eum occidi'.
[5] Ibid. 1. 54: 'qua vi senatorem perspicui generis interficeret'.
[6] Ibid. 1. 55.

The question here was one of seduction achieved by magic,[1] and, certainly, in the case of the *nefariae artes*, interrogation under torture *was* prescribed.

Now that we have seen what a weak character Aginatius was and how far Ammianus has deviated from the path of objective truth, we will listen to the text of the final act of this blood-and-thunder play:

'Doryphorianus journeyed, as bidden by Maximinus, with all possible despatch to Rome, and, setting to work on his inquisition, began most eagerly to seek opportunity to compass the destruction of that senator of famous rank without any external assistance. Finding that Aginatius had been already long ago seized and that he was being detained in his villa, he arranged for a personal interrogation of Aginatius and Anepsia, who had already been charged with the offence. He chose the dark and awful hour of midnight, as reason then is paralysed by fear. Among countless other examples, I may quote Ajax in Homer, who prefers to die by day, in order not to have to endure above all else the worse terrors of the night. As the judge—or, rather, the godless assassin—regarding only his promise [to Maximinus], sharpened all the points of the accusation and had arranged to proceed by examination under torture, he ordered the band of executioners to enter. To the tune of the dreary rattling of their chains the slaves, begrimed with dirt, were tortured almost to death to ensure their master's ruin; the whole procedure is forbidden by our mild laws in charges of seduction. When at last the mortal pains had extorted from one wretched slave girl a few confused words, he announced, without further testing the value of the confession, that the sentence of death was to be carried out on Aginatius without delay; no one took the slightest notice when Aginatius appealed in a loud voice to the names of the Emperors, but he was at once seized and put to death. By the same sentence Anepsia was executed. Such were the monstrous deeds of Maximinus, partly done in his own person, partly through his hirelings, when he was at a distance, and the Eternal City wept over the pitiful event. . . .'[2]

Let us not for a moment forget the alibi that the historian has already given: 'of all this we have no reliable proof'.

Putting aside this false and artificial moving picture inspired by hate, let us try to grasp the less sensational truth. Maxi-

---

[1] Ammianus xxviii. 1. 50: (on Anepsia, the widow of Victorinus): 'adpetitam se nefariis artibus, vim in domo Aginati perpessam, asseveravit'.

[2] See Note 26, p. 136.

minus, who was undoubtedly a very able and energetic administrator—Ammianus admits that he had had a moderate education[1]—began his career as an advocate, then attained the governorship of Corsica and Sardinia and, after that, that of Etruria;[2] on 17 November we find him in 366 A.D. still in this post;[3] but by 19 March A.D. 370,[4] he is *praefectus annonae* in Rome. At first, it appears, even the high aristocracy was contented with him,[5] but, as the result of an accident with which he had no concern, he came into conflict with the great families.

'The ex-vicarius Chilo and his wife, Maxima, brought an accusation before Olybrius, who in those hard times was governor of the city, to the effect that their lives were being assailed by means of magic. They succeeded in getting the persons under suspicion—the organist, Sericus, the strong man, Asbolius, and the soothsayer, Campensis—arrested at once and thrown into chains. But when, as a result of the long and serious illness of Olybrius, the affair cooled down, the complainants, impatient of the delay, put in a plea that the criminal charge should be transferred to the *praefectus annonae*, and, to secure a quick decision, their request was granted.'[6]

'When, in the course of the preliminary inquiry, he had tested the matter at many points'—so Ammianus goes on to report of Maximinus—'and certain persons, cruelly harassed by the tools of torture, had mentioned by name certain aristocrats, asserting that they had used some worthless clients, already known as evil-doers and informers, to hire the services of the deadly masters of magic for their designs, that judge, ripe for hell-fire, was beside himself and sent a malicious report to the Emperor, insisting that these dangerous offences, which were being so

---

[1] Ammianus xxviii. 8. 6.

[2] The evidence was last collected by W. Ensslin, *RE*. Suppl. v. 663 ff. Cf. also L. Cantarelli, *La diocesi Italiciana*, 1903, 117, 209, 216.

[3] *Cod. Theod.* ix. 1. 8.

[4] Ibid. xiv. 17. 6; cf. also Seeck, *Regesten*, 32. 9; E. A. Thompson, op. cit. 138 ff.

[5] Ammianus xxviii. 1. 6: 'egitque . . . iam inter exordia cautius'.

[6] Ibid. 1. 8–10: 'Chilo ex vicario et coniux eius Maxima nomine questi apud Olybrium, ea tempestate urbi praefectum, vitamque suam venenis petitam adseverantes, impetrarunt ut hi quos suspectati sunt, ilico rapti, conpingerentur in vincula, organarius Sericus, et Asbolius palaestrita et aruspex Campensis. verum negotio tepescente ob diuturnam morborum asperitatem, qua tenebatur Olybrius, morarum inpatientes hi qui rem detulerunt, libello petiverunt oblato, ut examinandum iurgium praefecto mandaretur annonae, idque studio celeritatis concessum est'.

freely practised in Rome, could only be tracked down and avenged by severe punishments. Valentinian, on receiving this information, fell into a passion and being in such matters a bitter rather than an austere enemy of the offences, he ordered by a single edict that, in such cases, which he arrogantly confused with deliberate high treason, all those who by our time-honoured legal system and by the principles laid down by the deified Emperors were exempt from examination under torture, might now be brought to the bench of torment, if the course of the investigation demanded it.'[1]

It appears, then, that these scandals in Rome were suddenly revealed by an accident, and also that neither Valentinian nor Maximinus was responsible for the latter being entrusted with the investigation. The proposal was laid before the Emperor by Olybrius[2], whilst the Emperor sent Leo, the *notarius*, as *adlatus* to serve beside the *praefectus annonae*. The scandal was, indeed, on a colossal scale. As we shall see later, the hocus-pocus of magic and witchcraft was regarded as a deadly and revolting truth, and the mere fact that such low practices should be used in senatorial circles aroused general consternation. And not without reason. Even we can share the feelings; for it makes no difference that we know these magic rites to be silly and harmless nonsense: the intention to do injury was certainly there.[3] It is not true either, that Valentinian 'arrogantly confused' the charges of magic with high treason. For, in the case of Hymetius,[4] our author himself defines the object of the magic sacrifices as the conciliation of the Emperor, and in the opinions of the day that constituted high treason. This will not have been the only case. Even Ammianus is not at all

---

[1] See Note 27, p. 136.

[2] Cf. Ammianus xxviii 1. 12 (about these affairs): 'Maximino Romae agere disposito pro praefectis, sociavit ad haec cognoscenda ... Leonem notarium, postea officiorum magistrum'; ibid. 13: 'auxit obstinatum Maximini ingenium ad laedendum ... adventus collegae similis et litterarum cum ampla dignitate dulcedo', who, in place of the 'vicarius' Aginatius recommended the 'praefectus annonae' as Chilo too had proposed; ibid. 32: 'Aginatius ... dolens ... in examinandis causis Maximinum ab Olybrio sibi praelatum, cum esset ipse vicarius Romae'.

[3] Ammianus, it is true, tries to hush up the prevalence of these rites in the circles of the aristocracy (cf. above, pp. 71 f.), but the fact emerges clearly from the rest of the text, for example, xxviii. 1. 17–23, 26, 29.

[4] Ibid. 1. 19–21.

indignant at the prosecution for these capital charges:[1] what does seem to him outrageous is that the mighty oligarchy should be attacked.[2]

Maximinus was not a man to be scared of his own shadow. We shall see later how he almost compassed the ruin at the hands of the executioner of the Bishop of Rome, a man as powerful as himself, as the real instigator of the riots that had caused the death of hundreds. The Emperor—decent, puritanical, a bitter enemy of crimes and abuses,[3] always concerned for the purity of public life[4]—was convinced that Maximinus was the most suitable man to be chosen for the ugly task[5] and placed himself unreservedly behind him.[6]

The trial of these shocking cases was not as devilish and illegal as Roman circles maintained. There were some acquittals,[7] and Maximinus himself in some cases mitigated the iron severity,[8] which really corresponded to the letter of the law, and so did the Emperor, when he referred to the Senate for decision a case which unquestionably called for the death penalty; the Senate then reduced the punishment to banishment.[9] And, when the Senate sent three of its distinguished members, Praetextatus, the former *praefectus urbi*, Venustus, the *ex-vicarius*, and the consular Minervinus on a mission to court, to ask that the punishments should not be assessed with excessive severity,[10] and that men of senatorial rank should not be submitted to torture,[11] the Emperor gave way and granted their petition.[12]

---

[1] Cf. also E. A. Thompson, op. cit. 101 ff.   [2] See Note 28, p. 136.

[3] Ammianus xxx. 9. 2: 'domi castus et foris', ibid. xxviii. 1. 11: 'vitiorum inimicus'; *Epit. de Caes.* 45. 5: 'infestus vitiis'.

[4] Ammianus xxvi. 4. 2; xxx. 9. 3; Zosimus iv. 16; *Cod. Theod.* i. 6. 6, &c.

[5] In connexion with the cases of magic in question Ammianus (xxx. 8. 13) says: 'iudices numquam consulto malignos elegit'.

[6] Ibid. xxviii. 1. 21: 'haec Valentinianus relatione iudicum doctus, asperius interpretantium facta, vigore nimio in negotium iussit inquiri'.

[7] Ibid. 1. 27.

[8] Ibid. 1. 40: 'uno quasi praecipuo tolerabilis, interdum enim exoratus parcebat aliquibus'.   [9] Ibid. 1. 23.

[10] Ibid. 1. 24: 'ne delictis supplicia sint grandiora'.

[11] Ibid.: 'neve senator quisquam, inusitato et inlicito more, tormentis exponeretur'.

[12] Ibid. 1. 25: 'hacque libertate emendatum est crudele praeceptum'.

The Senate regarded the severe punishment of the cere-
monial ritual of the *haruspices* as a great injustice because they
saw in it an insult to paganism. We shall later have to go into
this point at greater length.[1] The Emperor, on the other hand,
only persecuted the searchers of entrails for magic; in an ex-
ceptionally courteous letter[2] he assured the fathers of his religious tolerance.[3] Meanwhile Maximinus was advanced to be
vicarius[4] and, immediately after this imperial edict, Valentinian called him to his Court and made him *praefectus praetorio Galliarum*.[5] It was probably just his inexorable severity
shown in those cases that made Valentinian remove him from
Rome to a higher post, thus implying still more imperial favour;
but it was at the same time an attempt to do something to
conciliate the Senate. The same purpose was served by an edict
of 6 December A.D. 371, in which Valentinian hands over
charges of magic, in which senators are involved, to the *praefectus urbi*, with the comment that, if he cannot settle them,
he is to refer them to the Emperor himself.[6] This implies the
important negative principle that, in such affairs, it shall not

Ammianus here draws a pitiful picture of the Emperor (ibid. 25): 'qui cum
intromissi in consistorium haec referrent negantem Valentinianum, se id
statuisse, et calumnias perpeti clamitantem, moderate redarguit quaestor
Eupraxius'. Such conduct in the Emperor is incredible, nor can we believe
that Eupraxius took it on him to contradict his master in the presence of the
envoys of the Senate. Such behaviour will not fit in with that manly character, which, by its imposing superiority, won the admiration of contemporaries
on all occasions, as Socrates states, *H.E.* iv. 1: καὶ ἀεὶ τῆς παρούσης τύχης μείζων
ἐφαίνετο.   [1] In the volume mentioned above, p. 6.
    [2] A phrase out of this document may be preserved in the *constitutio* of the
Cod. Theod. ix. 38. 5 (cf. Mommsen, *Theod. libri* xv, p. 496 and Seeck, *Reg.*
248): 'indulgentia, patres conscripti, quos liberat, notat nec infamiam criminis
tollit, sed poenae gratiam facit. in uno hoc aut in duobus reis ratum sit: qui
indulgentiam senatui dat, damnat senatum. dat. XIIII. Kal. Iun. Tre(viris)
Gr(ati)ano A.II et Probo conss.' We take this to be a phrase of courtesy,
which might go on into praise. Gothofredus, who thinks otherwise, is followed
by L. A. A. Jouai, *De magistraat Ausonius*, 1938, 95.
    [3] *Cod. Theod.* ix. 16. 9 from 19 April A.D. 371.
    [4] When Ampelius was *praefectus urbi*. Cf. Ammianus xxviii. 1. 22; *Epist.
imper.* 12 (*Corp. Script. Eccl. Lat.* xxxv. 59).
    [5] Ammianus xxviii. 1. 41. The earliest mention of him as *praefectus prae-
torio Galliarum* is in *Cod. Iust.* vi. 22. 7, dated 7 August A.D. 371. Cf. Seeck,
Reg. 131. 29, and J. R. Palanque, *Essai*, 40 ff.   [6] See Note 29, p. 137.

rest with the *vicarius* to direct the proceedings against the aristocrats, or, to put it plainly, that it is not the confidants of the Emperor but the lawful governors of Rome, favourable as they are to the great families, that shall decide. All the stranger is it to find that, even after the departure of Maximinus, cases of magic and seduction, arising in aristocratic circles, continued just as before to be conducted by the *vicarii* who succeeded him.[1] Is not the explanation that the city prefects were too cowardly? In the case of Olybrius himself it is by no means out of the question that his 'illness' was no more than an excuse for evading the awkward and odious affair. To assume that the Emperor broke his word is impossible for us who know his character.

The excitement caused by these scandals had thoroughly intimidated the noble society of Rome.[2] They were on their knees to Maximinus.[3] Some of them fled or hid, so that the Emperor had to issue a special edict, threatening punishment to any who concealed them.[4] As far as we can judge, the number of victims may really have been considerable.[5] Even sons of the noblest families could be found among them. We already know of Aginatius and Alypius of the family of the Anicii, and of Probus, the head of the house, who did not venture to defend him; the Ceionii and Decii, too, to take another example, lost

[1] Ammianus xxviii. 1. 43 ff.: 'et ... tamen ... inmorabimur paucis, quae per iniquitatem curantium vicariam praefecturam in urbe, contra quam oportuerat, gesta sunt, quia ad nutum Maximini et voluntatem, isdem ministris velut apparitoribus gerebantur'; 46: '... cruento enim certamine cum Maximino velut antepilano suo contendens, superare eum in succidendis familiarum nobilium nervis, studebat [Simplicius]'.

[2] Ibid. 1. 16: 'in quorum miseriis, velut sui quisque discriminis cernens imaginem, tortorem et vincula somniabat, et deversoria tenebrarum'; 38: 'ortuque nobiles inculti videbantur et anxii'. This fear echoes again in Ammianus' own recollections (xxviii. 1. 2): 'ac licet ab hoc textu cruento gestorum exquisite narrando, iustus me retraheret metus, multa reputantem et varia, tamen praesentis temporis modestia fretus, carptim ut quaeque memoria digna sint, explanabo'.

[3] Ibid. 1. 38: '[ortu nobiles] salutantes humum paene curvatis contingentibus membris'.

[4] See Note 30, p. 137.

[5] Hieron. *chron.* A.D. 371 (p. 246, 5 Helm): 'Maximinus praefectus annonae maleficos ab imperatore investigare iussus plurimos Romae nobilium occidit'.

members of their family[1] though some of the banished succeeded later in coming back and recovering their possessions.[2] The nobility were afraid of total ruin if things continued to take this course.[3]

But it was not only with the higher aristocracy that Maximinus—and with him the Emperor who backed him—came into conflict, but also with the Roman Church, as E. Caspar has recently discovered.[4] The preliminaries were as follows. A split in the Roman Church had occurred in the year A.D. 355— in the very bosom of the Catholic community of the Nicene Confession of Faith. One side had chosen the deacon, Felix, as bishop in place of the banished Liberius and the result of this double election led, in A.D. 366, after the death of Liberius, to a new duplication of bishops, through the simultaneous election of Damasus and Ursinus. It came to serious and bloody riots between the two parties. The chief fight took place when the adherents of Damasus besieged their rivals in the Basilica of Liberius (Santa Cecilia in Trastevere); the dead alone were counted to well over one hundred. The civil authorities were in an uncommonly difficult position. On the one hand, there was the policy of the Emperor, who declined on principle to interfere in the internal affairs of the Church; on the other, there was the fact that both sides were orthodox and belonged to the Nicene Confession, as did the Emperor himself. The Pannonian Viventius, the *praefectus urbi*, tried to give moderate support to Damasus, who seemed to be the stronger, by sending his rival into banishment; but he would not interfere in the riots and waited outside the walls to see how things would turn out. Only Ursinus and a few of his confederates were banished; but, after a bare year, when tempers seemed to have cooled down, they returned home—only under threat of the severest punishment from the Emperor if they should

[1] Seeck, *Symm.* praef., pp. 174 ff. Symmachus may have had personal reasons for being angry with Valentinian, as the Emperor had ordered the banishment and confiscation of goods of his father-in-law, Orfitus (Ammianus xxvii. 3. 2 and 7. 2). Cf. Seeck, *RE*. iv A. 1145 f.

[2] Cf. E. A. Thompson, op. cit. 104, 107.   [3] See Note 31, p. 137.

[4] E. Caspar, *Zeitschr. f. Kirchengesch.* xlvii, 1928, 178 ff.; the same, *Gesch. d. Papsttums*, i, 1930, 203 ff., 593. I have nothing to add to the conclusions of Caspar, which I am reproducing here; I think, in this larger context, they may gain in importance.

ever again break the peace. It was no mere chance that as *praefectus urbi* at that time had been chosen Praetextatus, one of the spiritual leaders of the aristocracy, a pagan, who was not restricted in his actions by the discipline of the Church. When mass butcheries broke out again, he once more banished Ursinus from Rome and placed the meeting-places of his adherents in the hands of Damasus. When they still continued to hold their separate services outside the walls and the bands of their enemies again proceeded to attack them, the rival Pope, Ursinus, was deported to Gaul and his adherents were driven out of the vicinity of Rome. Still, the after-effects of the conflict continued to make themselves felt. And no wonder. No one had tried to settle the bloody conflict by way of the police and the criminal law. The desperate Maximinus even ventured to meddle with this nest of hornets too when the defeated faction turned to him as umpire.

In A.D. 370 or the next year[1] a Jew named Isaac, who had received baptism but had afterwards returned to his old faith, laid a criminal charge against Damasus[2] as the real criminal in the murders that had occurred at the double election of popes.[3] He was put up to do this by Ursinus,[4] who had just returned from Gaul, where he had been banished, to Milan[5] and was now

[1] Cf., for example, H. Lietzmann, *Gesch. d. alten Kirche*, iii, 1938, 221 ff. and *RE*. xiii. 98 ff. (with lit.); E. Caspar, *Gesch. d. Papsttums*, i, 1930, 188 ff. with a list of the ancient sources and modern literature.

[2] We only know the story from the allusions contained in the letter of the Council held in Rome in A.D. 378 by the Emperors Gratianus, Theodosius, and Valentinianus II (Mansi, *Sacr. concil. nova et amplissima coll.* iii. 1762. 624 ff.). Cf. also the answer of the Emperors to the letter (*Epist. imper.* no. 13: *Corp. Script. Eccl. Lat.* xxxv. 1, 1895, 54 ff.). On the critical interpretation of these texts see E. Caspar, *Gesch. d. Papsttums*, i, 1930, 594 and *Zeitschr. f. Kirchengesch.* xlvii, 1928, 189.

[3] E. Caspar calls our attention to the fact that, as early as A.D. 367, the adherents of Ursinus were calling his opponent, Damasus, *auctor scelerum* and *homicida*: *Epist. imper.* i, c. 9 and 12.   [4] See Note 32, p. 137.

[5] This conclusion had already bèen drawn by J. Wittig ('Papst Damasus I', *Röm. Quartalschr.* Suppl. xiv, 1902, 11 ff.) from a passage in the acts of the Council of Aquileia (Mansi, op. cit. iii. 621). Cf. E. Caspar, op. cit. 184, n. 4. Cf. also Ambr. *ep.* 11: 'turbare (Ursinus) Mediolanensem ecclesium coeta detestabili moliebatur . . . nunc ante synagogae foras, nunc in Asianorum domibus miscens occulta consilia'.

trying indirectly to evict from his seat the rival whom he could not overthrow directly. Maximinus handled the proceedings with the same iron and merciless severity with which he had dealt with the charges against the aristocrats, and the Church was as furious at the examination of clerics under torture as the Senate had been at the similar ill treatment of its members.[1] Maximinus, on the grounds of the imperial mandate issued on the occasion of the illness of the *praefectus urbi*, Olybrius,[2] or perhaps of a special commission already received at the time of the city prefecture of Ampelius, was competent, in fact, to proceed against the Bishop of Rome.[3] He was, it appears, determined to destroy Damasus.[4] 'But now he exceeded his competence, which was, to decide the case in person for the Emperor. Sentences of death, in the case of senators, had to be submitted to the Emperor for his personal decision and the same course was followed in capital offences affecting Bishops.'[5] In the meantime, Churchmen of the Nicene Confession had intervened at Court in favour of Damasus;[6] and, even apart from that, it is easy to see that the Court would not allow him to fall. Damasus was the man of the Government's choice, that one of the rivals in whose support the authorities had from the first mobilized all the resources of the State. It would have been a political absurdity to drop him because of a charge subsequently staged by the rival party.[7] But, even so, this criminal charge was a serious blow to Damasus, and it became necessary to rehabilitate him morally by a recall of the Council in A.D. 378, to wipe out the shame and degradation which the proceedings

[1] See above, pp. 65 ff.

[2] See E. Caspar, *Zeitschr. f. Kirchengesch.* xlvii, 1928, 184.

[3] Cf. ibid. 178 ff.

[4] Rufin. *H.E.* ii. 10: 'quae res factione Maximini praefecti . . . ad invidiam boni et innocentis versa est sacerdotis'.

[5] E. Caspar, *Gesch. d. Papsttums*, 1930, 204 ff.

[6] See Note 33, p. 138.

[7] E. Caspar, *Zeitschr. f. Kirchengesch.* xlvii, 1928, 188: 'Damasus war der Mann der Regierung, derjenige der beiden Rivalen um den römischen Bischofstuhl, für dessen Unterstützung der Staat seine Autiortät und seine Machtmittel von Anfang an eingesetzt hatte. Es wäre eine politische Inkonsequenz gewesen, ihn nachträglich durch eine von der Gegenpartei inszenierte Kriminalklage zu Fall bringen zu lassen.'

of Maximinus had brought upon him.[1] At the same time Valentinian, doubtless provoked to it by Maximinus, had done terrible despite to Damasus in yet another affair.

It was only at the very end of the fourth century that the male members of the noble families began, in any numbers, to forsake the religion of their ancestors. But ever since the age of Constantius II their women had been the chief supports of the Church of Rome, and their pious gifts had brought the Church important material possessions. The bishop and his clergy—Damasus not the least among them[2]—exploited this source of revenue with regularity and energy. In this way they withdrew important inheritances from the rich families. Against these practices an edict of 30 July A.D. 370 took up a rudely uncompromising attitude. It was addressed by the Emperor to Damasus direct and he was required to have it read aloud in all the churches of Rome. The edict forbade priests, under heavy penalties for disobedience, to visit the houses of widows or orphan minors, or to receive any kind of material benefit from the women whom in the name of religion they deluded. It declared every will of this kind invalid and, for the future, confiscated all such bequests.[3]

As we have already seen, Valentinian, on the plea of the Senate, had ordered examination under torture in the criminal cases of the aristocrats at Rome to be suspended, or, it might be, restricted. Again, in this case of the sentence proposed on Damasus, he took up a different position from Maximinus. That meant that the Pannonian courtiers had failed to extend the brutal legislation of the age to the privileged social classes of Rome. Maximinus had even to leave Rome—no doubt under the combined pressure of the priests and the aristocracy—even if that meant kicking him upstairs.[4]

Especially noticeable from our point of view is the circumstance that a community of interests now developed between

---

[1] Ibid. 189 ff., 196.   [2] See Note 34, p. 138.

[3] See Note 35, p. 138.

[4] E. Caspar, *Zeitschr. f. Kirchengesch.* xlvii, 1928, 189, n. 2: 'Possibly there is a connexion with the call of Maximinus away to another post and the quashing of his sentence in the case of Isaac by a higher authority.' But that was only one of the factors against him.

the aristocracy, mainly pagan, and the Roman Church in opposition to Valentinian and his people, an alliance which, taken together with the complete tolerance of the Emperor, gave the pagan religion of the State in Rome time to draw breath. The two disputed elections to the papacy had already turned the energies of the Roman Church in on itself and had diverted them from the fight against the pagans, and now the feeling might develop between Christian and pagans that, in some respects, they were dependent on one another. This was the atmosphere in which the pagan prefect of the city and the Pope could bandy jests with one another. The pagan prefect answers the attempt of the Pope to convert him with the words: 'Make me Bishop of Rome and I will become a Christian forthwith.'[1]

As long as Valentinian lived, the noble circles in Rome only ventured to scoff at him as blood-thirsty and avaricious[2] in secret; at Court Petronius Probus refused outright to come to the aid of his fellow nobles in the Roman scandals.[3] Symmachus, too, on 23 February A.D. 369, and 1 January 370, delivered joyful panegyrics on the Emperor whom he hated for his severity.[4] But when, in the autumn of A.D. 375, the Emperor, while staying in Brigetio in Pannonia, his homeland in the narrower sense, died of a sudden stroke; when the sword, that alone might have checked that terrible shock of the northern peoples, Huns, Alans, and Goths, that was just about to begin, slipped from his hand, reaction at once raised its head against those who represented his spirit.

A sharp change of policy now occurs, and we may realize it from a letter which a leading senator, Q. Aurelius Symmachus, wrote to Ausonius, the Gallic poet, whom Valentinian had chosen to be tutor to his son, Gratian, and to whom he had then given the high dignity of *quaestor sacri palatii*,[5] in order that he might in that capacity display the brilliance of his style in the composition of the imperial edicts. From his letter it appears that,[6] as early as 1 January A.D. 376, the Senate re-

---

[1] Hieron. *Adv. Iohann. Hierosolymitanum* 8 (= Migne, xxiii. 397 f.).

[2] Ammianus xxviii. 1. 20.   [3] See above, pp. 79 ff.

[4] Seeck's edition, pp. 318 ff.

[5] O. Seeck, *Q. Aur. Symmachi quae supersunt* (*Mon. Germ. Hist., auct. ant.* vi. 1), 1883, p. lxxix, n. 357.   [6] Symm. *ep.* i. 13.

ceived the special message (*oratio*) of Gratian, who had been Augustus since A.D. 367 and now, after the death of his father, took over the rule of the West. The courier travelled night and day[1] and thus might, at the speed of those days, arrive with the news of Valentinian's death from Brigetio in Pannonia to Treveri, and straight on from there to Rome[2] between 17 November and the New Year. That means that there can have been no negotiations between the Court at Treviri and the Senate preceding the imperial message (*oratio*) and, therefore, that this new policy of friendship to the Senate, so solemnly announced by Gratian, reveals the threads of a plot that must have been spun before. Symmachus also emphasizes his old friendship with Ausonius and their interchange of letters.[3] Their common cultural ideals may explain why—though the senators are pagan, but Ausonius, nominally at least, a Christian —in this respect, that is to say, in opposition to the mighty Pannonians, they are of one mind. Indeed, their common interests make this quite intelligible. We already know how the senators felt, and from Ausonius, too, we have expressions which show that he—in relation to his imperial benefactor— was completely in harmony with them.[4] Here, then, we can grasp that new political coterie (*factio*) which now, in place of the Emperor and his men, seized the government in the name of an Emperor hardly more than a child.

The *oratio* of Gratian to the Senate, which arrived on 1 January, as we can see from the exaggerated letter of thanks from Symmachus, not only filled the senators with good hopes and joy,[5] but actually implied a basic improvement in their position. They at once exploited this to the full,[6] for, in their

[1] Symm. *ep.* i. 13. 2: 'tabellarius vigiliarum fessus'.

[2] O. Seeck has already noted this, op. cit., prol. lxxxi.

[3] *Ep.* i. 13. 1.

[4] Ausonius, *Grat. act.* i. 3 (written to Gratian at the end of A.D. 378): 'palatium, quod tu, cum terribile acceperis, amabile praestitisti'. To the situation of the senators in the days before and after the death of Valentinian the passage in the same context applies: 'curia honorificis . . . laeta decretis, olim sollicitis maesta quaerimoniis'.

[5] Symm. *ep.* i. 13. 1: 'domini nostri Gratiani caelestis oratio'.

[6] Ibid. 3: 'dic mihi, inquies, . . . quid nostri patres super ea oratione senserunt? novimus bona nostra complecti'.

answer, in the midst of all their expressions of thanks, they gave vent to their complaints too.[1]

In the third century, when the Emperors were as a rule proclaimed by their troops at a distance from Rome, they hastened to bring their elevation to the knowledge of the Senate by a courteous obeisance before it. Apparently the fourth century continued the practice, but it had now sunk to be a mere empty courtesy. But on this occasion there was no question of a new Emperor (for Gratian had been in office since A.D. 367), but only of the death of the senior Emperor and of the succession of his son to his primacy in rank. The proclamation of a change of direction in government, then, was no usual formality but a political manifesto, implying the sudden increase in the political weight of the Senate.

Symmachus, too, ventured in his answer, in veiled but unmistakable terms, to censure the rule of the father in the presence of his son. When he wraps the new régime of Gratian in the cloak of the symbolism of the Redeemer, as applied to the pagan Roman Emperor, and glorifies it as a new Age of Gold,[2] he is implying that the dark night, which is so sharply contrasted with the dawn of the new age, is nothing other than the reign of Valentinian.[3] The 'general blessedness' (*felicitas publica*), which has now arrived,[4] is nothing but the revival of the Senate, whilst the mention of the 'other ways',[5] contrasted with the blessed age of the good Emperors of old, cautiously but plainly pillories the government of the dead Emperor.

[1] Symm. *ep.* i. 13. 4: 'audisti omnia sed summo tenus ore libata; monumenta curiae nostrae plenius tecum loquentur. ubi cum plura scripta repereris', &c.

[2] Ibid. 2: 'novi saeculi fata'; cf. on the coins of Gratian the legend GLORIA NOVI SAECULI. The *saeculum* is, of course, the Age of Gold; cf. Symm. *or.* 4. 15: 'haec est illa Latii veteris aetas aureo celebrata cognomine, qua fertur incola fuisse terrarum necdum moribus offensa Iustitia. pie regimur', &c.

[3] *ep.* i. 13: 'primores kalendas Ianus aperibat. frequens senatus matutine in curiam veneramus, priusquam manifestus dies creperum noctis absolveret. forte rumor adlatus est, sermonem desiderati principis multa nocte venisse. et erat verum, nam tabellarius vigiliarum fessus adstabat. nondum caelo albente concurritur; luminibus accensis novi saeculi fata recitantur. quid multa? lucem, quam adhuc opperiebamur, accepimus.'

[4] Ibid. 1.   [5] Ibid. 3: 'mores alii'.

And the man to whom the letter was addressed was the spiritual author of the imperial message of the New Year. 'For now Ausonius did not only determine the style of the imperial decrees, he also fixed their contents.'[1] Soon afterwards, on 9 January, Symmachus delivered a speech in the senate-house in which he was so sure that the Senate had gained the upper hand—as a result, again, of the New Year proclamation—that he ventured to accuse Valentinian of envy and suspicious malice.[2]

The omnipotence of Ausonius is revealed on every hand. So, for example, in the administration: the organization of the posts of professor in the cities of Gaul and their liberal pay[3] was one of his first concerns.[4] Whereas Valentinian had always proclaimed his inexorable severity, the new constitutions emphasize their humane and gentle tendency.[5] This was all very fine. But, in other places, the spirit of Ausonius finds less pleasing expression. He gets the young Emperor to appoint his son at once *proconsul Africae*[6] and then *praefectus praetorio*; he gets his son-in-law made *vicarius Macedoniae*, then, in place of his son, *proconsul Africae*; he has the rank of *praefectus praetorio* conferred on his father; the grandson of his sister becomes *comes rerum privatarum*, then *praefectus urbi*; while

---

[1] O. Seeck, *Gesch. d. Unt. d. ant. Welt*, v. 41. According to Seeck (*RE*. iv A. 1147) Symmachus was entrusted (as on a later occasion) with the reading of this letter; but I can find no indication of this in the text. I regard it as equally doubtful whether the Constitutions, collected in Seeck (*Regesten*, 105; *Cod. Theod.* xv. 1. 19, ix. 1. 13, x. 19. 8; *Cod. Iust.* iii. 24. 2) are certainly fragments of this New Year's speech. See also L. A. A. Jouai, *Ausonius de magistraat*, 1938, 167, who, opposing Seeck, wishes to take them as parts of a second *oratio*; still less can I accept this view.

[2] See Note 36, p. 139.

[3] *Cod. Theod.* xiii. 3. 11 (23 May A.D. 376).

[4] Other evidences of his spirit that appear in his edicts have been collected by O. Seeck, *Q. Aur. Symm. quae supersunt*, prol., p. lxxix.

[5] Seeck, *RE*. vii. 1834, quotes in this context the passages in Ausonius, *Grat. act.* 15. 71 and 16. 72, as well as the words of Symmachus, *or.* 4. 15. A good example of this practice is to be seen in the edict, *Cod. Theod.* ix. 19. 4, on the mitigation of procedure in cases of forgery of wills: 'removebitur itaque istius lenitate rescripti praecepti superioris austeritas', in contrast to which he emphasizes the *humanitas* of his own attitude (16 April A.D. 376).

[6] Seeck, *RE*. vii. 1834.

he himself advances from *quaestor sacri palatii* to *praefectus praetorio*—to say nothing of more distant relatives whom he placed in more or less notable positions, so that in the Western half of the Empire every single post of any importance came at a stroke into his family,[1] and they were able to enrich themselves to an incredible degree. Behind the fine-sounding phrases gross selfishness lay concealed.

The reaction after the reign of Valentinian was introduced by a general amnesty and by various alleviations of conditions—all at the initiative of Ausonius, to make the new régime popular.[2]

'Up to then the demands of the State chest had been enforced with great severity', writes Seeck; 'now, all arrears of taxation were cancelled and the lists that recorded them were burned in public in the market-places.[3] Valentinian had occasionally ordered the execution of defaulting debtors; Gratian now forbade the use of torture against them.[4] The banished were recalled, prisoners held for examination were released, confiscated property was restored to the heirs of those whom Valentinian had executed.[5] In short, it was made clear to the people at all points that the rule of iron cruelty was now at an end, and that in deliberate contrast to it lovely clemency had mounted the throne.'

But this pretty programme was soon forced by the new movements of the peoples on the frontiers to give place to the habitual exercise of the dreadful screw of taxation.

When Ausonius and his friends moved Gratian to issue his edict, by which information given by a slave against his master

[1] Seeck, *Symm.*, prol., p. lxxix.

[2] That Gratian made these arrangements in obedience to his teachers (εὐπείθεια τοῖς διδασκάλοις) is attested in the twelfth speech of Themistius (pp. 171D and 173A Harduin); that among the teachers of Gratian we have, first and foremost, to think of Ausonius has been emphasized by Seeck, *Gesch. d. Unt. d. ant. Welt*, v. 440 on p. 40. 29 and 441 on p. 42. 11.

[3] Ausonius, *Grat. act.* 16. 73–4; Them. *or.* 13, p. 175C (Hard.).

[4] *Cod. Theod.* ix. 35. 2: examination under torture is allowed against decurions only in cases of *crimen maiestatis*, not of offences against taxation; from the use of the leaden whip only the *decemprimi* are relieved; cf. Them. loc. cit.

[5] Them. *or.* 13, pp. 171C, 174B, 175A, 177A–C (Hard.); Ambros. *De obitu Theodos.* 52 = *P.L.* xvi. 1466; Ausonius, *Grat. act.* 15. 71; Ammianus xxix. 3. 7.

was not to be admitted, but the informer was to be burned alive, and even the freedman was to be punished with death if he accused his patron, they undoubtedly intended a slap at the judges in the *causes célèbres* of Rome.[1] And when the edict was sent direct to Maximinus, we see in it a pinprick specially meant for the confidant of Valentinian, whose power was now on the decline. But the edict did not mean any serious protection for the nobles, as the case of high treason was expressly excepted—and that was always the most dangerous charge against them. Another imperial constitution directed against the rapid increase of charges of high treason did no more than assuage the fears of the aristocracy.[2]

The entourage of Gratian induced him, on 11 February A.D. 376, to reinforce the privileges of the senators in criminal law. The provincial governors may indeed conduct a preliminary inquiry in cases of senators, but they are required to furnish a report to the Court or the prefect on the spot—strictly, not on the case, but on the person. In the circle that most concerned the senators, that of Rome and its environs, the *praefectus urbi* with a Commission of Five gives the verdict. We can understand, then, what unjust privileges were thus secured to the nobles against those of lower rank when the case was conducted at home by those who shared their rank and interests.[3] There is no doubt, too, that this order prevented for the future any *vicarius*, hostile to these class interests, from meddling in criminal charges against the senators, as Maximinus had done.[4] Soon afterwards, on 4 January A.D. 377, the Emperor solemnly forbade the interrogation under torture of senators: this is another epilogue to the battle against the champions of Valentinian.[5] Perhaps, too, a deliberate contrast to the spirit of

---

[1] *Cod. Theod.* ix. 6. 1–2 (15 March A.D. 376).

[2] Ausonius, *Grat. act.* 15. 71; Seeck, *RE.* vii, 1835, calls attention to the passage. The new regulation of the relations at law of the *praefectus urbi* and the *praefectus annonae*, *Cod. Theod.* i. 6. 7 (13 July A.D. 376) is probably an after-effect of the activities of Maximinus, although it only refers to the supply of necessaries of life and does not touch the men's competence in criminal law.   [4] See Note 37, p. 139.

[3] Cf. the commentary of Gothofredus on this law.

[5] *Cod. Theod.* ix. 35. 3 = *Cod. Iust.* xii. 1. 10 (4 January A.D. 377): 'impp. Valens Gr⟨at⟩ianus et Val⟨entini⟩anus A.A.A. ad Gracchum praefectum urbi.

Valentinian is to be seen in that edict which gives a slight advantage in precedence to civil authorities in matters of jurisdiction by placing the *vicarius* above the military *comes rei militaris*.[1]

Whereas Valentinian as Emperor had deliberately shunned Rome, Gratian seized the first opportunity to visit the Eternal City in the summer of A.D. 376, and there celebrated, we must suppose (as usual a year in advance), the popular festival of his ten years of rule.[2] It was customary on such occasions to invite famous orators to deliver panegyrics on the Emperor, sonorous speeches that were the greatest delight that the cultured public of the age could imagine. Now, at the invitation of Gratian,[3] the famous orator and philosopher of Constantinople, Themistius, came to Rome, and his speech, entitled Ἐρωτικός,[4] enthusiastically praised Rome and the Senate, taking sides with a surprising frankness for the pagan ideals of the old civilization. We shall see later what capital for the maintenance of the threatened old religion the defenders of the *mores maiorum* made out of this victory of the Senate and out of the new honours paid to the national traditions of Rome. But, after three short years, the paths of Gratian and that ancient and honourable corporation separated.

One of the circumstances characteristic of this change of political direction was, of course, a change of personnel in high places. The young Emperor, immediately after the death of his father, changed all his *praefecti praetorio*;[5] we have seen above how Ausonius and his kin seized all the fat appointments. Among the new men the appearance at the Court of Treviri of the brother and son-in-law of the *magister equitum*, Theodosius, is most interesting; these two men, Eucherius and

---

severam indagationem per tormenta quaerendi a senatorio nomine submovemus. dat. prid. non. Ian. Tre(viris) Gr(ati)ano A. III et Merobaude conss.' Cf. A. Ehrhardt, *RE*. vi A. 1775 ff. (with further literature).

[1] *Cod. Theod.* i. 15. 7 (6 January A.D. 377).

[2] Cf. Seeck, *Die Briefe d. Liban.* 303; the same author in *RE*. vii. 1835.

[3] Them. *or.* 31, p. 429. 5 ff. Dind.: ἱκανός μοι Γρατιανὸς σεμνυνόμενος πρὸς Ῥωμαίους ὡς αἴτιος αὐτοῖς γεγονὼς τῆς ἐμῆς ἐπιδημίας.

[4] *Or.* 13, pp. 198 ff. Dind. On the date see H. J. Bouchery, *L'Antiquité classique*, v, 1936, 191 ff.

[5] J. R. Palanque, *Essai . . .* , 1933, 48 ff.

Syagrius, in the posts of *comes sacrarum largitionum* and *magister officii*, will probably have been responsible later for Gratian's choice of the younger Theodosius as his colleague.[1] The elder Theodosius, one of the most distinguished generals of Valentinian,[2] who had been executed at the very end of his reign,[3] had been on very good terms with Symmachus[4] and certainly had a general sympathy for the senatorial circles,[5] while his ruin,[6] with that of many men of mark,[7] was due to a collision with the clique of Maximinus. Should we not see in the sudden and decisive fall of the Pannonian *factio* of Maximinus after the death of his imperial master traces of a conspiracy of the Gallo-Hispanic *factio* of Theodosius against Valentinian and his agents? A strong piece of evidence supports this supposition. The way in which the elder Theodosius disposed of Firmus and the Count Romanus in Africa reveals him as an astute and formidable opponent and his whole clique seems to have been

[1] O. Seeck, *Gesch. d. Unt. d. ant. Welt*, v. 124 and 479. The execution of Valentinus, the brother-in-law of Maximinus, was carried out by Theodosius the Elder; cf. W. Ensslin, *RE*. vii A. 2274 f.

[2] See R. Egger, *Byzantion*, v, 1930, 9 ff., with further literature; cf. also G. de Sanctis, *Riv. di Filol.* lxii, 1934, 53 ff.; E. A. Thompson, op. cit. 89 ff., 93 ff., 100 f., 106 f., 129 f., 138 f.

[3] Thus W. Ensslin, *RE*. v A. 1943 ff., rightly against R. Egger, op. cit. 25 ff., who would postpone his fall to the time of Gratian. So does A. Hoepfner, *Rev. ét. lat.* xiv, 1936, 119 ff., who is wrong in thinking that, at the beginning of A.D. 376, Gratian still stood under the influence of Maximinus. Cf. above.

[4] Symm. *ep*. x. 1. 1–2. Cf. Seeck, *Symm.*, prol. xlii ff.

[5] Cf. Ammianus xxix. 5. 4, whose sympathies naturally also go out to the ancestors of the reigning dynasty.

[6] Hieron. *chron*. A.D. 376, the marginal note of a contemporary: 'Theodosius Theodosii postea imperatoris pater . . . multorum per orbem bellorum victoriis nobilis in Africa, factione eorum periit qui et ipsi mox caesi sunt, id est Maximini ex praefecto'. The note is certainly authentic. Cf., for example, R. Egger, op. cit. 25; Oros. vii. 33. 7, speaks of his ill-wishers who brought about his fall. Some acute remarks are to be found in E. A. Thompson, *The Historical Work of Ammianus Marcellinus*, 1947, 93 ff., 138 ff.

[7] Hieron. *chron*. A.D. 376, says that with him *plurimi nobilium occisi*. His son too was in danger of his life; cf. Ambros. *De obitu Theod.* 53: 'portavit iugum grave Theodosius a iuventute, quando insidiabantur eius saluti qui patrem eius triumphatorem occiderant. portavit iugum grave, quando subiit pietatis exsilium', &c.

no better. And the sudden advance of adherents of Theodosius at Court, in connexion with that senatorial reaction which, immediately after the death of Valentinian, snatched power in the West by a sudden stroke, also does invite one to ponder.

In the award of the dignity of consul, too, a new order is revealed. For the year A.D. 377, at the petition of the Senate, the father of Symmachus, former *praefectus urbi*, was designated ordinary consul;[1] in 379 the son of another great Roman family, Olybrius, became consul beside the still omnipotent Ausonius. In a word, even if the German generals—in this case Merobaudes—are not excluded, yet senators and civilians again share in this much coveted honour.

In this air the confidants of Valentinian, of course, could not breathe. The men of the new *factio* wanted their places. They probably could not yet induce the young Emperor to dismiss Maximinus.[2] But disputes soon arose between Maximinus and the all-powerful clique of Ausonius, which aimed at vexing and, if possible, damaging the hated *praefectus praetorio*.[3] Maximinus defended himself with energy and gave clear expression to his feelings,[4] and this led to his dismissal. On 16 April A.D. 376 the Court of Treviri is still addressing an edict to him,[5] but not long afterwards he had fallen.[6] The collaboration of the ruling clique at Court and of the Senate (of Ausonius and Symmachus, that is to say) is also shown when the Senate sends an embassy accusing Maximinus because of the sentences that he had given in the scandalous cases at Rome, and Gratian now ordered his execution with a severity usually reserved for cases of high treason.[7]

---

[1] Symm. *or.* iv and Seeck, *Symm.* prol. xliii.

[2] See Note 38, p. 139.

[3] For example, with the edict, *Cod. Theod.* ix. 6. 1–2. Cf. Seeck, *Gesch. d. Unt. d. ant. Welt*, v. 42.

[4] Symm. *or.* 4. 11: 'alienorum simulatione criminum Maximinus fidem fecit suorum. vestra aestimatio sit, qualis fuerit in ceteros, quem ipsi rerum domini tyrannum paene estis experti. urgebat enim novo fastu patientiam regiam et praefecturae suae putabat esse dispendium, si quid licuisset imperio'; Ammianus xxviii. 1. 57: '. . . Maximinus sub Gratiano intoleranter se efferens, damnatorio iugulatus est ferro'.   [5] *Cod. Theod.* ix. 4. 1.

[6] O. Seeck, op. cit.; W. Ensslin, *RE*. Suppl. v. 664; J. R. Palanque, op. cit.

[7] See Note 39, p. 139.

They then extended their operations to include the two former *vicarii urbis*, who had carried on after Maximinus the charges against the aristocracy of Rome. The death sentence on Simplicius was carried out in his native land, the charge against Doryphorianus was tried in Rome; he was then taken to Gaul and there put to death under horrible tortures.[1]

Gratian, in a solemn address from the throne, gave the Senate to understand that he intended to remedy their grievances.[2] With the reading of this address he entrusted Symmachus.[3] This distinction again illustrates the part played by the leading spirit of the pagan nobles in the events of the day.

The Senate, of course, celebrated the fall of its hated Pannonian rivals. It was, naturally, more guarded and cautious in its rejoicings over the fall of the régime of Gratian's father,[4] but it was all the louder in its jubilation over the fall of Maximinus and his friends,[5] and, at the same time, it exulted at the sudden growth of its political influence and power. The senators felt that in Gratian they had a man after their own hearts.[6]

The old ambition of the Senate to rule the world, which for a long time—and particularly in the recent past—had had to be more or less repressed, took on a new lease of life.[7] Symmachus hymns the restoration of the ancient *libertas*—he now takes it to mean that the Senate has gained the upper hand.[8]

[1] Ammianus xxviii. 1. 57: 'sed vigilarunt ultimae dirae caesorum. namque ut postea tempestive dicetur, et idem Maximinus sub Gratiano insolenter se efferens, damnatorio iugulatus est ferro; et Simplicius in Illyrico truncatus, et Doryphorianum pronuntiatum capitis reum, trusumque in carcerem Tullianum, matris consilio, princeps exinde rapuit, reversumque ad lares, per cruciatus oppressit inmensos'.

[2] Symm. *ep.* x. 2. 2: 'domine Gratiane . . ., quoniam ita animatus es, ut cum reipublicae medicinam facis, operam meae vocis accersas. tu nobis publicas turbas in tranquillum redegisti'.

[3] Ibid. 2. 1: 'ut sacrae orationi vestrae lector adhiberer'.

[4] See Note 40, p. 140.

[5] See Note 41, p. 140.

[6] Symm. *ep.* x. 2. 1: 'amore . . . quo summates viros plerumque dignamini (sc. Gratiane)', ibid. 3: 'senatus ius antiquum obtinet'.

[7] See Note 42, p. 140.

[8] Symm. *or.* 4. 13: 'bene igitur aput vos locata est tutela rei publicae: pacem innocentiae reddidistis, abrogata est externis moribus vis nocendi, crevit principatus, quia liberis imperatis; tantum potestatibus quantum

The barbarian Maximinus of Carpic, i.e. Dacian descent (and, with him, his master, who was equally reputed to be a barbarian) has fallen,[1] classical culture—or, rather, the virtuosity of the rhetorician, which late antiquity confused with the other—is now at home at Court. Symmachus writes to Gratian as to a 'man of taste', not in the usual tones of official propriety but as a literary magnate of the age to the patron of the Muses.[2] In this is involved, of course, quite a lot of flattery for Ausonius, the author who rules the docile young Emperor, but even more we see the hope which regards the partisanship of the Emperor for the Senate as a victory of the national ideals in the field of religion too. The pagan reaction exulted over the elaborate rhetorical antitheses and the elegant turns of Symmachus. We see the movement which had been free to gain strength through the toleration of Valentinian in the circles of the Roman aristocracy and which was now saturated with political ambitions; and, for the moment, it was not troubled by the Church, which, as we have seen, had been its companion in sufferings and almost an ally against Maximinus and was thus fettered for the moment by the compelling force of the danger which they had surmounted in common. But this blissful honeymoon of Emperor and Senate was not to last long.

On the frontiers dark and heavy clouds were gathering, even while the spokesman of the Senate was still trumpeting the rise to power of the new national ideals. 'The source of this ruin, the origin of our manifold afflictions which the wrath of Mars called down on us, setting the world ablaze', writes Ammianus,[3] in solemn tones, as if describing some magnificent funeral, 'was as I learn, as follows. The people of the Huns, hardly known to our ancestors, which lives in the marshes of the Maeotis near the ice-bound ocean, exceeds all imaginable degrees of barbarism. . . . This unstable and undisciplined race of men, burning with the lust to plunder foreign lands and rob neighbours, had

---

legibus licet'. Ibid. 4. 7: 'inter senatum et principes comitia transiguntur: eligunt pares, confirmant superiores. idem castris (at Court, that is to say) quod curiae placet: quis hoc non putet orbis terrarum esse iudicium?'

[1] Symm. *or.* 4. 13: 'abrogata est externis moribus vis nocendi'.

[2] See Note 43, p. 140.

[3] Ammianus xxxi. 2. 1, 12.

now reached the Alans.'[1] Ammianus goes on to record how the Huns carried the Alans away with them and ousted the Gothic peoples from their homes; 'the report went abroad that a new type of mankind was breaking out of some concealed nook of earth and was ravaging and destroying everything nigh, like a storm descending from the mountains' height'.[2] And into the Roman Empire, too, came the tidings of terror—that 'over the whole extent (of the northern frontier) from the land of the Marcomanni and Quadi to the Pontus a vast mass of barbarian peoples, hitherto hidden from our view, had been dislodged by a sudden thrust from its habitations and was now swarming along the banks of the Danube . . .'.[3]

It was in the spring of A.D. 376 that this happened. A little later and all the horrors of murder, robbery, and incendiarism filled the Balkan lands.

[1] Ibid. 12.   [2] Ibid. 3. 8.   [3] Ibid. 4. 2.

V

THE LATE CLASSICAL IDEAL OF CULTURE IN CONFLICT WITH THE ILLYRIAN MILITARY SPIRIT

THE friction between Valentinian and his Pannonians and the Senate was only a new revelation of an old contrast which had arisen over a century before when the Illyrian soldiers had ousted the senatorial governors from the higher military[1] commands. In them Rome the city and Rome the Empire were confronted as enemies. The noble body which fed on the prestige of the ancient past was compelled to give way to those who incorporated in themselves the supreme political power of the present. The Pannonians could say what Saint Augustine said later to the proud bearers of the Roman tradition: 'What can Rome be but the sum of all Romans? For we are not speaking now of stones and beams, not of great masses of houses and mighty walls . . . .'[2]

The Emperors, keeping their eyes on realities, had from the first opposed the idea that the sons of the mother-city had a sole and unique right to claim full recognition. While they kept on extending the privileges of the Roman citizen to ever wider circles and were thus always approximating to an equal treatment of all regions and all peoples of the Empire, raising the provinces and subordinating the point of view of Rome and Italy to the interests of the provinces as a whole, yet they continued formally to surround the Senate, that had built the world Empire, with its ancient honours. So, even under changed conditions, the Senate could continue to dream of the *res publica*

---

[1] M. Vogelstein, *Kaiseridee — Romidee*, 1930, 4 ff., 8 ff., 29, n. 3; J. Vogt, *Orbis Romanus*, 1929 = *Vom Reichsgedanken der Römer*, 1942, 170 ff.; J. Gernentz, *Laudes Romae*, Diss. 1918, 49 ff.; M. Gelzer, *Gemeindestaat und Reichsstaat*, 1924 = *Vom römischen Staat*, I. 6 ff.; E. Korneman, *Stadtstaat und Flächenstaat* (reprinted from Ilberg's *Neue Jahrbücher*, xxi. 233 ff.); R. Heinze, *Über die Ursachen der Grösse Roms*, 1925, &c.

[2] Augustine, *sermo* 81. 9 (Migne, *P.L.* xxxviii. 505): 'Roma enim quid est nisi Romani? non enim de lapidibus et lignis agitur, de excelsis insulis et amplissimis moenibus'.

and its own sovereignty. The institution of the monarchy with its four hundred years of existence was still, in its eyes, a usurper. The Senate never assesses the merits of the provincials from the angle of history; anything they give is but obligatory service, due to the Queen of the World, *domina Roma*.

There was a reason for the wide importance of the ideals that the Senate represented. The *curia* was commonly regarded as the true guardian of the canonical ethical tradition of the ancients, and so the conception that it entertained of national morality was in many respects binding on those persons and grades of society that counted in politics. The rhetorical culture, then completely dominant, steadily held up the ideal of a Fabricius, a Cincinnatus, a Cato as a model for men of breeding to follow, and history, dependent on rhetoric, applied the same measure to the statesmen of the past and held them up as a mirror for the present to copy.

It would be interesting to bring to light the roots of this moral conception. They are actually to be found in the political attitude of Augustus. For while he definitely stabilized the monarchy by securing for it the necessary military power and its legal and administrative requisites, yet the first *princeps* always did obeisance to the Senate, the bearers of Republican *libertas*; and, in this sphere too, his conduct became a cornerstone of political correctitude. In the realm of history Tacitus has given a classical mould to this attitude. To suit the requirements of that Senate, which till recently had really been so powerful, he erects a Republican back-stage, in front of which his actors can play their historical parts. With suspicious care he observes how the individual monarchs behave as 'first citizens'; but with him that does not mean—far from it—that they talk like true democrats to the 'man in the street', but rather that they treat the senatorial class as their peers.[1] The Senate still contrived to maintain its old claims; for the writing of history remained in the hands of senators even when the political importance of the body was steadily declining and the reins of the army were falling out of its hands, when Rome ceased to be an imperial residence and therewith lost its power.

[1] Cf. my remarks in *Römische Mitteilungen*, xlix, 1934, 25 ff. and the appendix (below, pp. 126 f.).

But it is not our task to trace this process in detail. It might, of course, happen that history was written by men who were not members of the Senate, but, even then, the irresistible force of literary form still secured canonical validity for the old ideas. Later again, the senatorial reaction in the fourth century, which I am trying to elucidate as a phenomenon of the greatest historical importance, filled the old forms, so long grown stiff, with new life. We will now illustrate this process by a few examples.

About the middle of the fourth century a little work, composed of short biographies of Emperors, came into being. It is not in our possession today,[1] but, in the decades following, a whole series of authors, mostly senators, pirated it ; in the main they seem to have taken over its material, adorned it with their own flowers of style, and then presented it under their own names. Of this company was Sextus Aurelius Victor, a literary man of North Africa, who rose from low degree to high imperial dignities and whose little book, entitled the *Caesares*, appearing at the end of the reign of Constantius II, is brimful of senatorial arrogance. When this same Victor—whether copying from his source or airing his own views—preaches against the caprice of the soldiers (*militaris potentia*), he may be speaking of the past, but he is striking at the present. 'At this', writes Victor about the murder of Domitian and his condemnation by the Senate, 'the soldiers more concerned for their own advantage than for the damage to the common weal were furious, and rebelled, in their usual way, and demanded the execution of those responsible for the murder of the Emperor. Reasonable people'—in the vocabulary of Victor, that always means the Senate—'had very great difficulty in pacifying them so that they finally acquiesced in the decision of the optimates. But they were still preparing to fight, for the change of government (that is to say, the end of the tyranny) distressed them, because they had lost their rich prizes from the imperial bounties.'[2] Of Pertinax

---

[1] A. Enmann, 'Eine verlorene Geschichte der röm. Kaiser und das Buch *De viris illustribus urbis Romae*', *Philologus*, Supplementband iv, 1884, 337–501.

[2] Victor, *Caes.* 11. 9–11: 'quo moti milites, quibus privatae commoditates dispendio publico largius procedunt, auctores necis ad supplicium petere more

Victor says: 'He was shamefully murdered, at the instigation of Didius, by the soldiers; for nothing; will content them now that they have sucked the world dry and brought it to perdition.'[1] 'The soldiers are a type of man who always covets gold and is never good and true unless he stands to gain by it', so he sighs on another occasion.[2]

Victor (and his source) carefully follows the process by which the soldiers wrenched from the Senate the supreme military command recognized by law (*imperium*) and, with it, the choice of Emperors. He does not realize that this process had begun with Caesar and had long been complete, and that, in all the changes of succession in the third century, only a few traces of constitutionalism maintained a feeble existence.[3] He supposes[4] that it was only after the death of Probus (not so very long, then) that the *militaris potentia* succeeded in removing this foundation-stone of sovereignty from under the feet of the Fathers. When he laments this supposed sudden loss of the Senate's power and waxes indignant that, even to this day, no scion of the senatorial class can be a commander of great armies, he is really depicting the fight of the nobles for power in A.D. 360—only a few years before the accession of Valentinian. It was not the conduct of the Emperor that engendered the storm that we have described—he only enabled the old conflict to burst forth once more.

It would be instructive to follow the epitomes of Victor and his companions and trace the leading threads in the history of the third century, but we must content ourselves with a few

---

suo seditiosius coeperunt. qui vix aegreque per prudentes cohibiti tandem in gratiam optimatum convenere. neque minus per se moliebantur bellum, quod his conversum imperium maestitiae erat ob amissionem praedarum per dona munifica.'

[1] *Caes.* 18. 2: 'eum milites, quis exhausto iam perditoque orbe satis videtur nihil, impulsore Didio foede iugulavere'.

[2] *Caes.* 26. 6: 'milites . . . genus hominum pecuniae cupidius fidumque ac bonum solo quaestu'. Cf. also, for example, 34. 1: 'militesque quos fere contra ingenium perditae res subigunt recta consulere'; 35. 7: 'inter quae avaritiam peculatum provinciarumque praedatores contra morem militarium, quorum e numero erat (Aurelianus), immane quando sectabatur'.

[3] See my arguments in *Röm. Mitt.* l, 1935, 43 ff.

[4] *Caes.* 37. 6.

hints. First of all, Victor waxes indignant at the proclamation of Maximinus Thrax (A.D. 235), the first common soldier to be raised to the throne.[1] From him he dates the decline of Rome and declares desperately that, from then on, vice won all along the line, when even the vilest born—*horrendum dictu* (he was one of them himself!)—were admitted to public life.[2] He then sets up a political signpost for his age, inscribed: 'Every Emperor, who dares to infringe the (supposed) sovereign rights of the Senate, can only have been a ghastly tyrant or an un-educated barbarian.'[3]

Victor is very conscious—and in this he merely represents the ordinary mentality of the Senate—that, even if he has to crawl on his belly before the living Emperor, he is the judge of Emperors once dead, able, under his cloak of historian, to express an unbiased opinion on their policy, according as it has been favourable to the Senate or not.[4] In him as in the short historical epitomes of similar content, it is essential to note how large a part of the few lines of these imperial biographies is taken up with the definition of their attitude to the Senate. The part is so large that, in its one-sidedness, it completely distorts the picture of the Empire. In judging his Emperors he employs formulas that show whether they were descended from noble senators from consular families or not.[5] At the same time he deals nasty blows at those Emperors who rose from below.

'From these things I see clearly', says Victor, 'that, to the best of my judgement, even the lowest man, especially if he rises high, knows no bounds to his arrogance and greed. That is why, for Marius in the days of our ancestors and for (Diocletian) in this present age, the old ways of life are no longer good enough; for such souls, only just escaped from starvation, who have never known power, are insatiable. And I am astonished that it is the aristocrats who are usually regarded as arrogant, when they really have some right to console themselves with their prestige for those vexations of the patrician families that give them no rest.'[6]

[1] See Note 44, p. 141.   [2] See Note 45, p. 141.
[3] See Note 46, p. 141.   [4] Victor, *Caes.* 33. 24.
[5] Eutropius 9. 19: 'Diocletianum, . . . virum obscurissime natum', 9. 21: 'Carausius . . . vilissime natus', &c.
[6] Victor, *Caes.* 39. 5–7: 'quis rebus, quantum ingenium est, compertum

In the eyes of men like these the tyrant is the Emperor who ventures to order the execution of noble senators, a good Emperor is one who never raises a finger against them.[1] The compiler of the *Historia Augusta*, whose historical judgement reflects the views of the noble society of Rome in the late fourth century, is never tired of stressing that a good Emperor is he who is never weary of flattering the Senate: in the ideal picture of his perfect Emperor, Alexander, this is one of the chief excellencies on which he is always enlarging.[2]

Among the formulae characteristic of the minor historical catechisms in Latin of the fourth century, there is another one that exalts the Emperors and dignitaries of senatorial extraction as representatives of *humanitas*, while the soldier Emperors of low birth and their entourage of similar quality, are pilloried by way of contrast, as clumsy, stupid peasants or even, in unjustified hatred, are called savage barbarians.[3]

For this, too, there are earlier precedents. Cassius Dio Cocceianus, who came into serious conflict with the Pannonian soldiers under Alexander Severus, depicts the Pannonians as rough, wild brawlers,[4] writing disparagingly of their primitive conditions, in contrast to the sons of Italy and other civilized lands. The picture of the brave, but slow-witted, Illyrians is again drawn, not without prejudice, by Herodian.[5] The first

habeo humillimos quosque, maxime ubi alta accesserint, superbia atque ambitione immodicos esse. hinc Marius patrum memoria, hinc iste nostra communem habitum supergressi, dum animus potentiae expers tamquam inedia refecti insatiabilis est. quo mihi mirum videtur nobilitati plerosque superbiam dare, quae gentis patriciae memor molestiarum quis agitatur remedio eminere paululum iuris habet.'

[1] Eutropius, *Brev.* 7. 23 (on Domitian): 'interfecit nobilissimos e senatu'; 8. 4 (on Trajan): 'nihil non tranquillum et placidum agens, adeo ut eius aetate unus senator damnatus sit, atque is tamen per senatum ignorante Traiano'.

[2] Cf. the appendix, p. 126.

[3] Victor, *Caes.* 24. 9 (after Alexander Severus): 'inmissique in imperium promiscue boni malique, nobiles atque ignobiles, ac barbari multi'; again, on the laziness of the senators: 'munivere militaribus et paene barbaris viam in se ac posteros dominandi'.

[4] Cassius Dio lxxiv. 2. 2–4. Cf. Á. Dobó, *Inscriptiones extra fines Pannoniae Daciaeque repertae ad res earundem provinciarum pertinentes*[2] (Diss. Pann. i. 1), 1940, 26.   [5] Herodian ii. 9. 11.

imperator to come from Illyricum, the Thracian Maximinus, is called by a contemporary a half-barbarian, and out of this the compiler of the *Historia Augusta* creates a primitive savage.[1] Lactantius, the Christian rhetorician, borrows this conception of senatorial history[2] to hit out at those two terrible enemies of the Church, the Emperors Galerius Maximianus and Maximin Daia. He not only reviles them as uncultivated peasants coming straight from the woods in which they had fed their herds,[3] but calls them in so many words half-barbarous[4]—or even beasts in human form, escaped from barbary.[5]

The Pannonian Maximinus, the confidant of Valentinian, suffered the same fate. Symmachus nags at his barbarous ancestry, bringing to light his 'outlandish ways',[6] i.e. foreign origin.[7] The reproach of barbarism levelled at the Pannonians draws on other sources too—on the recollections of classical literature and on the fact that, four hundred years before, the Pannonian Illyrians and the Thracians had really been barbarians. Even the plain man in the Roman street was still feeding on the glories of the ancient past and, while conducting himself as that glory demanded,[8] certainly looked down on the provincial, if only because he was not 'metropolitan'. Even in

---

[1] See Note 47, p. 141.

[2] K. Roller, *Die Kaisergesch. in Laktanz*, de mortibus persecutorum, 1927, 32 ff.

[3] Lactantius, *De mort. pers.* 19. 6: 'Daia vero sublatus nuper a pecoribus et silvis, statim scutarius, continuo protector, mox tribunus, postridie Caesar'.

[4] Ibid. 18. 13: 'Daiam adulescentem quendam semibarbarum'.

[5] Ibid. 9. 2: 'inerat huic bestiae naturalis barbaries et feritas a Romano sanguine aliena: non mirum, cum mater eius transdanuviana infestantibus Carpis in Daciam novam transiecto amne confugerat'. That is to say, his mother was of provincial descent, from Roman Dacia: that is the whole basis of the invective. See also ibid. 23. 4 and 27. 9, and my comments on the passages in *Daci e Romani in Transilvania*, 1940, 30 ff. = *Századok*, lxxiv, 1940, 151 ff.

[6] Symm. *or.* 4. 10 and 13: 'externi mores'.

[7] See above, pp. 15 ff.

[8] Ammianus xxviii. 4. 28: 'nunc ad otiosam plebem [sc. urbis Romae] veniamus et desidem, in qua nitent ut nominibus cultis, quidam calceorum expertes, ut Messores Statarii Semicupae et Serapini, et Cicymbricus cum Gluturino et Trulla, et Lucanicus cum Porclaca et Salsula, similesque innumeri'.

Italy as a whole the pride of the motherland in its culture, in contrast to the peasant folk of the provinces, was not extinct. We find interesting evidence of this attitude on the gravestone of Anversa, on which a Pannonian who had found his way there humbly acknowledges his 'barbarian' origin, as though he were confessing a sin.[1]

Whenever we meet with abuse of the Emperors, officers, and civil functionaries deriving from Illyricum, we can generally detect in the background the fury of the senators at the 'new men' who intrude into the high places in their stead. But it is strange that the Christian Lactantius should repeat the complaints of the greatest enemies of the Church.[2] It is easier to understand how in the presence of Julian the Apostate, who fought in the name of the ancient culture against barbarism, scoffs could be uttered at the unpolished entourage of the Illyrian Emperors,[3] or when, in Saint Jerome,[4] we meet a reflection of the wrath of the senators at the uncouth figures (*agrestes*) who oust them from the consulship, or when Aurelius Victor is revolted when ignoramuses can reach the pinnacle of the civil career.[5]

It is not without interest to observe in Victor how futile it is to deride with him the non-senatorial Emperors as clumsy,

[1] I have to thank H. Fuhrmann (of Rome) for my knowledge of the little-known publication, which contains this long inscription (now in the Museum of Sulmona): G. Mancini, 'Iscrizione sepolcrale di Anversa', *Estratto d. Atti del Convegno Storico Abruzzese*, Molisano, 1931 (Casabordino, 1933). It is the gravestone of a certain (. . . M)urranus, who speaks of himself (l. 32) in the following terms: 'Murranus, nam ipsa miseria docet etiam barbaros scrivere', and again (ll. 36 f.) 'me . . . hominem barbarum, nat(um) Pannonium'.

[2] Lactantius, *De mort. pers.* 22. 4–5: 'eloquentia extincta, causidici sublati, iure consulti aut relegati aut necati, litterae autem inter malas artes habitae et qui eas noverant pro inimicis hostibusque protriti et execrati. . . . iudices militares humanitatis litterarum rudes sine adsessoribus in provincias inmissi.' We need hardly observe that all this is vastly exaggerated.

[3] See Note 48, p. 142.

[4] Hieron. *ep.* 66. 7. 3 (*Corp. Script. Eccl. Lat.* liv. 655).

[5] *Caes.* 9. 12, on the position of the *praefectus praetorio* (he links his reflections to the age of Vespasian, but he is really talking of the present): 'verum hac tempestate dum honorum honestas despectatur, mixtique bonis indocti ac prudentibus inertes sunt, fecere nomen plerique potentia vacuum insolensque miseris, subiectum pessimo cuique et annonae specie rapax'.

common yokels,[1] when he is often obliged to admit that they were not so bad after all. Let us listen to a few characteristic passages: 'He at once made Maximian, his loyal friend, Emperor, who, although only half educated, was a good soldier and kindly.'[2] In connexion with the elevation of Galerius and Chlorus to the rank of Caesar he writes: 'Their native land was Illyricum, and, although they had little concern with the higher culture, yet, having grown up between work on the land and the miseries of a soldier's life, they were very good for the State.'[3] Again he writes of the same Emperors: 'But they had such astonishing natural gifts that, if they had entered on their careers educated, so that their want of polish might not have been revealed, everyone would have taken them for men of the highest distinction. From this it becomes clear that education, elegance, and amiability are qualities absolutely necessary for Emperors, as without them the gifts of nature are, so to say, unkempt or even shaggy and as such are despised, while the same qualities won eternal fame even for Cyrus, the Persian king.'[4] In this last comment, it is true, he relapses into his usual tone; but, on the other hand, he declares openly of the Lords of the Tetrarchy: 'Their concord especially teaches us that intelligence and experience in decent military service, such as

---

[1] Victor, *Caes.* 24. 9 ff. (quoted below, p. 141, n. 45); ibid. 40. 17 (on the tyrant Alexander): 'agrestibus ac Pannoniis parentibus vecordior'; ibid. 41. 26: 'Vetranio litterarum prorsus expers et ingenio stolidior idcircoque agresti vecordia pessimus'. It is to be noted that *agrestis* and *Pannonius* here mean the same thing; it probably was already so in the 'Anonymus' of Enmann; cf. *Epit. de Caes.* 40. 10 on Herculius: 'ortu agresti Pannonioque', and also Ammianus xxvi. 7. 16, on Valens: 'Pannonius degener', and also below, p. 117.

[2] Victor, *Caes.* 39. 17: 'Maximianum statim fidum amicitia quamquam semiagrestem, militiae tamen atque ingenio bonum imperatorem iubet'.

[3] Ibid. 39. 26: 'his sane omnibus Illyricum patria fuit. qui quamquam humanitatis parum, ruris tamen ac militiae mise(riis) imbuti satis optimi rei publicae fuere.'

[4] Ibid. 40. 12–13: 'adeo miri naturae beneficiis, ut ea, si a doctis pectoribus proficiscerentur, neque insulsitate offenderent, haud dubie praecipua haberentur. quare compertum est eruditionem, elegantiam, comitatem praesertim principibus necessarias esse, cum sine his naturae bona quasi incompta aut etiam horrida despectui sint, contraque ea Persarum regi Cyro aeternam gloriam paraverint.'

they brought with them out of the school of Aurelian and Probus, are almost enough to ensure virtue.'[1]

Aurelius Victor is equally aware that the other side had its faults, and he comments on the senators—in the form of mild reproach, it is true: 'And, indeed, while they delighted in idleness and trembled for their riches and counted it more important than eternal life to guard and increase them, they themselves have paved the way for the barbarian soldiers to tyrannize over them and their children.'[2] In contrast to them, he admits of the soldier Emperors that: 'It is certain that experience of evils and need makes men efficient and shrewd, whilst, on the contrary, those who have never experienced anything unpleasant and judge every man according to his property and his gold, make a worse show.'[3]

Mamertinus, in the speech which he delivered before Julian the Apostate thanking him for the consulship, lets fall similar remarks. After the nobles who abase themselves in their contests for high office, the type of the coarse but decent official attracts sympathy: 'We have an entirely new class of men, whom the Emperor has admitted to his friendship: they are uncouth (so our smooth city gentlemen think), not over-polite, countrified; they dislike the complaisance of flatterers, but they recoil from touching another man's money as from an evil thing and they esteem the welfare of the State and the praise of their glorious master as the highest good.'[4]

Symmachus does much the same when, on 25 February A.D. 369, he delivers a solemn eulogy of Valentinian, as though

[1] Ibid. 39. 28: 'sed horum concordia maxime edocuit virtuti ingenium usumque bonae militiae, quanta his sub Aureliani Probique instituto fuit, paene sat esse'.

[2] Victor, *Caes.* 37. 7: 'verum dum oblectantur otio simulque divitiis pavent, quarum usum affluentiamque aeternitate maius putant, munivere militaribus et paene barbaris viam in se ac posteros dominandi'.

[3] Ibid. 39. 27: 'quare constat sanctos prudentesque sensu mali promptius fieri, contraque expertes aerumnarum dum opibus suis cunctos aestimant, minus consulere'.

[4] Mamertinus, *Grat. act.* 21. 2 (p. 147 W. Baehrens): 'tum aliud quoddam hominum genus est in amicitia principis nostri rude (ut urbanis istis videtur), parum come, subrusticum; blandimentis adulantum repugnat, pecuniae vero alienae tamquam rei noxiae tactum reformidat, maximas opes in rei publicae salute et gloriosa imperatoris sui laude constituit'.

he had never heard of the claims of his own class to appoint Emperors and exercise sovereignty:[1] according to him, the army, when it chose the Emperor, was a worthy and qualified electoral assembly (in the Republican sense); the age of the corrupt assemblies of citizens of the old days is over—and so let it remain, for 'public affairs cannot be decided on by those who are sunk in sloth',[2] and he recognizes that the leaders of the army can rightly make an Emperor; they are a 'senate that has taken the field'.[3] 'Those who bear arms should decide to whom the command of the army shall be entrusted.'[4] 'What matter that his true opinions did not square with his hypocritical declamations in this passage! He has to admit that the political organizations of the capital had sunk into disuse and were no longer equal to such a fateful decision.[5]

Such admissions were only made by senators under stress. The normal thing was for them to despise the actual balance of powers and go on singing the old, sweet song. And they were in some respect right to do so. It was an age in which abstract theory triumphed over reality. So it would be a grave mistake to suppose that such expressions of attitude in literature as we have quoted have no importance in the fields of reality.

Until you have learned to know the spiritual structure of the age you might, indeed, not share that opinion. You might question whether, in that world of growing corruption and barbarism, anyone had any taste or interest left for literary effusions. But we have to remind ourselves that literature was the very essence of the culture of late antiquity, that literature was founded on grammar and rhetoric, and that its aim was to realize the type of the ideal speaker.[6] We may sum up by

---

[1] Symm. *or.* 1. 9 (p. 320 Seeck): 'aderat exercitus . . . digna plane comitia tanti imperii principatu'.

[2] Ibid.: 'tibi habe, vetustas, redemptas saepe centurias et gratiosas Quiritium classes et tribus plerumque venales: negotia mandare nesciunt otiosi'.   [3] Ibid.: 'emeritum bellis virum castrensis senatus adscivit'.

[4] Ibid.: 'armati censeant, cui potissimum regenda arma credantur'.

[5] The passage has recently been handled by J. Straub, *Vom Herrscherideal der Spätantike*, 1939, 33 ff.; but I cannot entirely agree with his views.

[6] H. L. Marrou, *Saint Augustin et la fin de la culture antique*, 1938, 4, 85 ff. Cf. also G. Boissier, *La Fin du paganisme*, i⁸. 187 ff.; Seeck, *Gesch. d. Unt. d. ant. Welt*, iv. 169, &c.

saying that the age had no humanistic or scientific horizon, no historical culture, no system of thought based on ethnology or sociology, no clear definition of its attitude to natural science, to say nothing of technology—all it had was literature. The man of letters, trained in the classical dialectics, then, was the only type of educated humanity known.

That is why the Court, for the discharge of such tasks as demanded culture, regularly stuck to literary men—and stuck the faster the more their numbers decreased. It is true, of course, that it had long been the custom that the Emperors should appoint literary men, stylists of repute, to the post of *ab epistulis*, who had to draft the imperial letters.[1] But Suetonius and other celebrities, who reached this distinction from the time of Hadrian onwards, advanced no farther; whereas their successors in the fourth century, though far feebler than they in talent and style, not only attained the high positions of *magister memoriae* and *quaestor sacri palatii* whose task it was to present the imperial edicts in dazzling style, but often climbed to the prefecture or even to the consulship.[2]

As early as the time of Diocletian we can notice that it is not so much training in law as practice in literature and rhetoric that prepares the young aspirant for the official career and the high posts at Court.[3] Later, it is even more the representatives of *belles lettres* and poetry who come to the fore in this field.[4]

[1] Thus Seeck, op. cit. 189. Cf. H. Bardon, *Les Empereurs et les lettres latines, d'Auguste à Hadrien*, 1940; E. Malcovati, *Cultura e letteratura nella domus Augusta*, 1941, &c.

[2] In a later chapter we shall show from many examples that men of letters continued to count in official positions, and that Seeck (op. cit. 194 ff.) is wrong when he maintains that Ausonius was the last instance of literary merit earning high position. Cf. also H. L. Marrou, *Histoire de l'éducation dans l'antiquité*, 1948, 401 ff., esp. 413.

[3] See Note 49, p. 142.

[4] Firmicus Maternus (*Mathes.* ii. 29. 19) analyses a man's career on the grounds of astrology and says: 'honores illi maximos in IX loco in domo sua pleno lumine Luna constituta decrevit (praesertim quia in nocturna genitura conditionis suae secuta potestatem in decernendis honoribus habuit principatus): doctrinam etiam et tantam litterarum scientiam inmutatis domibus Saturnus Mercuriusque decreverunt, ut oratio eius ac stilus veteribus auctoribus conferatur'.

The politic reaction under Julian the Apostate, with its strong literary flavour, of course, assembled the trained artists in rhetoric around the Emperor; but the same had been the case under his predecessors.[1] Under Constantine the Court was already crowded with stylists of this type, who depended on their rhetorical training, and on it alone,[2] and many of them made their way up to the highest positions attainable by private individuals.[3] Symmachus speaks of it as a matter of course that literary erudition should often be the way to reach high positions,[4] and is indignant when a distinguished rhetorician could not get any higher than the governorship of a small province.[5] The professors of the High Schools of Constantinople, at the beginning of the fifth century, after twenty years' exemplary service reached the same rank as the *vicarii*.[6] In the fourth century it often happened that a man was adopted into the Senate of Constantinople or Rome simply and solely on the ground of his literary merits,[7] and that the experts in rhetorical culture attained great distinction and even practical recognition by just this kind of knowledge. The statutes of the Senate of Constantinople (of the year A.D. 361) contain the regulation: in the election of praetors ten senators, who have attained the ordinary consulship and the prefecture, must attend and with

[1] See Note 50, p. 142.   [2] See Note 51, p. 143.

[3] A single example will be enough; Ammianus xv. 13. 1–2: '. . . Musonianus . . . orientem praetoriana regebat potestate praefecti, facundia sermonis utriusque clarus. . . . unde sublimius quam sperabatur eluxit. Constantinus enim, cum limatius superstitionum quaereret sectas . . ., nec interpres inveniretur idoneus, hunc sibi commendatum ut sufficientem elegit: quem officio functum perite, Musonianum voluit appellari, ante Strategium dictitatum, et ex eo percursis honorum gradibus multis, ascendit ad praefecturam.'

[4] Symm. *ep.* i. 20: 'iter ad capessendos magistratus saepe litteris promovetur'.

[5] Id. *or.* 6. 3: 'quis credat, summatem facundiae diu inter fori ornamenta numeratum praesidialem dudum recepisse provinciam multoque itinere decurso ad honorem paene exiguum navigasse, cum plerique hominum viliorum prope ab summis potestatibus inchoarent?' The climax of the aspirations of the *literati* to power is shown by a fictitious acclamation in the *Vita Taciti* (4. 4): 'ecquis melius, quam litteratus imperat?'

[6] *Cod. Theod.* vi. 21. 1 (15 March A.D. 425).

[7] Themist. *or.* 26 (p. 393. 18 ff. Dind.). Of the individuals just mentioned we shall have to speak in the later part of these studies.

them 'the philosopher Themistius too must be present, as his knowledge enhances the value of the act'.[1] For this Themistius his rhetorical art was in itself enough to enable him to play a leading part in the Senate of the Eastern capital under a whole series of Emperors.[2] He calls himself a philosopher, it is true, but in reality he was no more than a rhetorician, with a taste for moralizing. But how enthusiastically does Constantius II celebrate him in a letter addressed to the Senate of Constantinople![3]

When we reflect that such unproductive men of letters could never have dreamed of being celebrated by an earlier Emperor in the Senate for their style—it would have seemed too completely ridiculous and impossible—we can estimate the degree of the change that had taken place. And this is not surprising. It was just the decline of culture that made it appear so precious in the eyes of the late Romans: what had once been the common property of so many, the everyday baggage carried by the broad masses of men of any education, had now become a rarity and therefore bore good interest. Not only poetry and stylistic prose, but even empty rhetorical declamation was now amazingly highly esteemed. The trickery of rhetoric with its worn commonplaces is now welcomed as a revival of the brilliance of the classical beauties of old, which themselves were regarded with the greatest admiration. The banality of this empty, swollen style was not felt. The number of those who could relish these titbits was steadily on the decline, and there was more danger of their vanishing altogether than of men becoming tired of them. No wonder that these men of letters, for all the meagreness of their talents, became incredibly arrogant and unmercifully despised all other mortals.[4]

---

[1] *Cod. Theod.* vi. 4. 12: '. . . Themistius quoque philosophus, cuius auget scientia dignitatem'.

[2] Themist. *or.* 31 (p. 426. 20 ff. Dind.): τεσσαράκοντα ἔτη ταῦτα σχεδὸν ἐτέλεσε λειτουργῶν ὑμῖν ἐκ τῶν λόγων καὶ πρεσβεύων ἐφεξῆς ὁπόσας αὐτοὶ ἴστε πρεσβείας οὐκ ἀτίμως οὐδὲ ἀδόξως οὐδὲ ἀναξίως τῆς ὑμετέρας χειροτονίας, τὰς μὲν καθ' ἑαυτόν, τὰς δὲ τοῖς ἀρίστοις ὑμῶν κοινωνῶν. The tone of self-confidence is characteristic of this orator. See below, pp. 116 ff.

[3] See Note 52, p. 143.

[4] E. Norden, *Die ant. Kunstprosa*, i. 241 ff.; O. Seeck, *Gesch. d. Unt. d. ant. Welt.* iv. 197 ff.

In this unhealthy atmosphere men of letters reached high positions of authority. 'Par là', writes R. Pichon most appositely,[1] 'comme par beaucoup d'autres traits, l'Empire du quatrième siècle rassemble à la Chine; les emplois y sont confiés à une aristocratie de "lettrés" ou de "mandarins". Cette comparaison, d'ailleurs, indique à elle seule le vice de cette conception. Quand la littérature a pour mission essentielle, de préparer au fonctionnarisme, ni l'un ni l'autre n'y gagnent beaucoup.'

Indeed, the great jurists of the beginning of the third century, who as chiefs of the imperial Cabinet and as commanders of the guard had to see that the imperial edicts were cast in the proper form—for the *praefectus praetorio* of the time had to perform this double function, not to bear the civil administration of the individual parts of the Empire—these would have been, indeed, astonished could they have read the letter of Symmachus which he addressed to the *magister memoriae*, Patricius. This letter reveals the fact that the main proof of fitness for this important office at Court consisted in the ability to produce fine flourishes of literary style.[2] It is no longer legal knowledge but acquaintance with the elaborate style then in fashion that gives the qualification for office. There was a corresponding change in the language of the laws as compared with older times. There, in the imperial edicts, where we expect the simplest and clearest formulation we meet only the sounding periods, with their weary, complicated clauses and their flowery vocabulary.[3] The men of letters have taken possession of the imperial Chancellory and from now on only those could draw up the imperial 'constitutions' who were able to produce in the sweat of their brow the unnatural expressions of the flowery style, while training in law fell into complete neglect.[4] These men of letters abused their position, and the formulation

---

[1] R. Pichon, *Les Derniers Écrivains profanes*, 1906, 78 ff.

[2] Symm. *ep.* vii. 60. 2: 'an ego adversum iudicium publicum provocem scriptis epistularum regiarum magistrum? nostrum est pastorales inflare calamos, tuum sacris tibiis carmen incinere; nos obtundit otium, te usus exercet.'

[3] We shall deal with this flowery style in greater detail later.

[4] See, for example, H. L. Marrou, *Saint Augustin*, &c., 114.

of official ordinances developed into a veritable argot, to which later jurists had to append elaborate explanations to make it intelligible.

To acquire the prose style of late Latin, with its refined clichés and its extravagances, was no simple matter. As the class of decurions, that is to say, the flower of the civilian population of the cities, had been ruined, it was possible to only a few, apart from the sons of the great senatorial landowners, to acquire the literary education on which it depended. The aristocracy, therefore, came to take all the greater places again in the administration, in which the use of the heavy literary style could not be avoided.

These circumstances may explain how, through the role of the literary virtuosos, the cultural ideals of late Rome could have such a decisive influence even at a Court where the direction lay in the hands of provincials and soldiers coming from Illyricum and other lands, to say nothing at all of those German generals[1] who were almost completely untouched by the Roman ideal and yet had to play such a fateful part in government and politics. The effects were deep in their scope.[2]

The educated classes regarded the Emperor, in his life and almost always in his conduct, as the incorporation of their ideal, and the Emperors, for their part, were compelled to come out as the defenders of ancient culture. This attitude bound them to the Senate in two ways: on the one hand, they were forced to be merciful to the senatorial class as the guardians of this cultural inheritance; on the other, they had to spare the traditions of the City of Rome, which were inseparable from them.

[1] When Sidonius Apollinaris, about the middle of the next century, enthusiastically praises the style in which the Gothic noble Arbogast writes his letters, a style in which the harmonies of Latium ring again and which is as sweet as the flow of the waves of the Tiber, he gives us one more example of the undiminished power of the conceptions of the fourth century in his age. See Sidonius, *ep.* iv. 17. 1 (p. 68 Luetjohann): 'urbanitas, qua te ineptire facetissime allegas et Quirinalis impletus fonte facundiae potor Mosellae Tiberim ructas, sic barbarorum familiaris, quod tamen nescius barbaris morum', &c.

[2] Joh. Straub (*Vom Herrscherideal der Spätantike*, 1939, 146 ff.) has recently dealt with these problems under the heading: 'Die Kaiser und die hellenistisch-römische Bildungstradition'.

These men of letters, consequently, appear as the representatives of a moral power, independent of any constraint that the Government can impose and ready, in case of need, to defy it.[1] In full consciousness of their weight and influence, they never cease to preach that the Emperors cannot maintain themselves without literature and rhetoric. It is one of the main tasks of the authors of the biographies of the Emperors and of the compendia that draw on them to illustrate this point by examples. They praise the culture of the first dynasty[2] and carefully chronicle the education, the knowledge, and the general cultural capabilities of the following Emperors.[3]

Of course, we must not take literally everything that they report of good or ill. As we have tried to show, with the aims that we have described they make it an essential characteristic of the good Emperor to be versed in literature or, at least, to support it, whilst lack of education is a main feature in the portrait of the tyrant. Partiality or hate, as the case might be, disregarding the truth about the reigns that they praised or condemned, represented the Emperor as a patron of culture or as a rough savage to suit requirements. Thus it often happens that we can trace two distinct valuations of one and the same Emperor.

We see this at once with the Lords of the Tetrarchy of Diocletian. Of Galerius Lactantius reports that, under him, 'rhetoric was ruined, lawyers were exiled, . . . literature was counted as a pernicious occupation and its practicians must be regarded as adversaries and enemies and be trodden under and excommunicated'.[4] The author of the *Epitome de Caesaribus*, too, scolds Galerius for his 'rude and boorish style of legislation, corresponding to his origin as a cowherd';[5] Victor calls the elder Maximian 'half a peasant'.[6] Eutropius[7] describes him as

---

[1] See Note 53, p. 143.   [2] See Note 54, p. 143.   [3] See Note 55, p. 144.

[4] Lactantius, *De mort. pers.* 22. 4, taken over word for word, for example, in the great and distinguished work of P. Monceau, *Hist. littéraire de l'Afrique chrétienne*, iii, 1905, 294.

[5] *Epit. de Caes.* 40. 15: 'Galerius autem fuit (licet inculta agrestique iustitia) satis laudabilis, pulcher corpore, eximius et felix bellator, ortus parentibus agrariis, pastor armentorum, unde ei cognomen Armentarius fuit'.

[6] Victor, *Caes.* 39. 17: 'semiagrestis'.

[7] Eutropius, *Brev.* 10. 3: 'civilitatis penitus expers'.

a 'man devoid of any culture', and Victor says that the whole gang were peasants.[1] But if we listen for a change to a contemporary from Gaul, the rhetorician Eumenius, there were never Emperors like those who furthered the study and recovery of the sciences and the art of speech, as Diocetian and his colleagues did.[2] Of the reign of Constantius Chlorus he draws a picture that suggests that Constantius had truly brought culture to its zenith.[3] And if, in the second half of the fourth century, Themistius, one of the most celebrated stylists in oratory, in a speech addressed to the Emperor Jovian describes the zeal with which the old Emperors supported the sciences, he mentions among them Diocletian, who had honoured his grandfather for his philosophical attainments.[4] A third variation is illustrated in the attitude of the *Epitome* to another member of the Tetrarchy; its author tries to stitch the two mutually exclusive verdicts together.[5]

Under Constantine we meet yet another inconsistency in the attitude of the monarchy to the ancient ideal of culture. As we read the compendia of history, so well adapted to the mean cultural needs of the age, the clear truth never appears that this great innovator had deserted to the side of the adversary of the whole of the ancient ideal of culture—to Christianity. Victor depicts Constantine—in the reign of his son, it is true— as a fine and polished man of culture, who was extolled heaven-high for this virtue[6] by his subjects, although, in spite of his

---

[1] Victor, *Caes.* 39. 26.

[2] Eumenius, *De instaurandis scholis* 5. 22–4: 'cui enim unquam veterum principum fuit curae, ut doctrina et eloquentiae studia florerent, quantae his optimis et indulgentissimis dominis generis humani?' [3] Ibid. 6. 1–4.

[4] Them. *or.* 5, p. 76. 23 ff. Dind.: ἐῶ τοὺς ἄλλους, ἀλλ' ὅ γε πάλαι τὴν ἐπωνυμίαν λαβὼν ἐκ ταὐτοῦ σοι θεοῦ τὸν ἀρχηγέτην τῆς ἐμῆς οἰκίας. See also *or.* 11, p. 173. 7 ff. Dind.: ἔναυλα δὲ ἔτι καὶ τὰ τοῦ Διὸς ἐπωνύμου πρὸς τὸν τηνικαῦτα φιλοσοφοῦντα ἐν Βυζαντίῳ.

[5] *Epit. de Caes.* 40. 18, on Daia: 'ortu quidem atque instituto pastorali, verum sapientissimi cuiusque atque litteratorum cultor, ingenio quieto, vini avidior'. See also, on the cultural aspirations of this Emperor, E. Stein, *Gesch. d. spätrömischen Reiches*, i, 1928, 135 ff.

[6] Victor, *Caes.* 40. 12 ff.: 'quare compertum est eruditionem elegantiam comitatem praesertim principibus necessarias esse. . . . at memoria mea Constantinum, quamquam ceteris promptum virtutibus, adusque astra votis omnium subvexere.'

imperial descent, he had been rather illiterate:[1] he was, first and foremost, a soldier, like his father and that father's colleagues in Empire. The *Epitome*[2] praises with enthusiasm his heavy and artificial literary compilations, just as Eutropius praises his civil spirit and his unselfish devotion to culture.[3]

The fact remains that this uneducated man on the throne was not able up to his very last years, up to the very end, to break with the ideal of classical culture. 'That famous Athens should elect him its *strategus*, as Pericles of old, was regarded by the Lord of the world as a great honour, and he rewarded the cheap flattery by feeding the mob of that decayed city at the expense of the State chest with yearly gifts of corn, notwithstanding that it was empty.'[4] It is true that he did not admire the ancient culture only for its outward show; the religious and philosophical speculations of the Neoplatonists exercised some influence on him and Platonic philosophers long abode beside him as his confidants.[5] About his support of literary culture, that is to say, of classical education, he himself waxes fervent in a letter that has come down to us;[6] he did, in

---

[1] Cf., for example, my remarks in *The Conversion of Constantine*, 1948, 20.

[2] *Epit. de Caes.* 41. 14: 'commodissimus tamen rebus multis fuit: . . . nutrire artes bonas, praecipue studia litterarum, legere ipse scribere meditari audire legationes et quaerimonias provinciarum'.

[3] Eutropius x. 7. 9: 'civilibus artibus et studiis liberalibus deditus'; Optat. Porph. *ep.* 6 (p. 38, E. Kluge): 'eius imperatoris testimonio, qui inter belli pacisque virtutes, inter triumphos et laureas, inter legum sanationes et iura etiam Musis tibi familiaribus plaudis, ut inter tot divinae maiestatis insignia, quibus et invictus semper et primus es huius etiam studii micat splendor egregius'.

[4] O. Seeck, *Gesch. d. Unt. d. ant. Welt*, i[4]. 53 on the basis of Julian, *or.* 1. 6. 9 (p. 19 Bidez). Cf. also Seeck, op. cit. i[4]. 469 on p. 53, l. 15.

[5] See my remarks, op. cit. *passim*, with further references to the literature. O. Schissel von Fleschenberg, *Klio*, xxi, 1927, 361 ff.; A. Piganiol, *L'Empereur Constantin*, 1932, 159 ff. Further references to the literature in *C.A.H.* xii, 1939, 797 ff. (collected by N. H. Baynes). I omit quoting here the praises of the Church Fathers.

[6] *Ep. Constantini ad Optatianum Porph.* 5 ff. (Opt. Porph. *Carm.*, ed. E. Kluge, pp. 40 ff.): 'defuit quorundam ingeniis temporum favor, qui non secus doctrinae deditas mentes inrigare atque alere consuevit. . . . saeculo meo scribentes dicentesque non aliter benignus auditus quam lenis aura prosequitur denique etiam studiis meritum a me testimonium non negatur. liber

fact, encourage efforts of this kind;[1] that means that under him, too, the influence of classical culture never ceased to affect the behaviour of the Emperor.

Licinius, the defeated adversary of Constantine, is, of course, branded as an arch-enemy of culture by the army of scribblers who are always ready to kick a dead lion.[2] As a matter of fact, there are indications that he was by no means unimpressionable in this respect.[3]

The sons of Constantine, the third generation of the family to sit on the throne, received a very careful classical education, and, earnest Christians though they were, encouraged rhetorical culture most warmly.[4] The letter sent by Constantius II to the Senate of Constantinople, recommending the election of Themistius as senator,[5] is a formal confession of faith in the higher culture, and itself, if he really composed it, gives a splendid example of fine literary education—classical education, of course, for at that time there was no other. In the same spirit Constantius takes care that only persons with a literary education shall be admitted to the Senate,[6] and he was the Maecenas of the celebrities of literature, even if they adhered to paganism.[7] We have tried to show elsewhere[8] how this influence of classical ideals compelled this bigoted Christian to come to terms with the national and pagan reaction of the West, led by the great senatorial landowners of the City of

assidue cursus orationibus fuit, eos vero, qui versibus dicerent, certis finibus lex metris statuta continuit', &c.

[1] *Cod. Theod.* xiii. 3. 1, for example.

[2] Cf., for example, *Epit. de Caes.* 41. 8–9: 'infestus litteris, quas per inscitiam immodicam virus ac pestem publicam nominabat, praecipue forensem industriam. agraribus plane ac rusticantibus, quod ab eo genere ortus altusque erat, satis utilis ac militiae custos ad veterum instituta severissimus.'

[3] Anon. post Dionem, frg. 14. 2 (*F.H.G.* 4. 199 = Cassius Dio, ed. Boissevain, iii, p. 748, no. 188).

[4] On Constans cf. Seeck, *Gesch. d. Unt. d. ant. Welt.* iv. 49.

[5] Themist., pp. 21 ff. Dind.

[6] Zonaras xiii. 11 (D. 3, p. 207 Dind.). Ephraem Syrus was quoted in this context by O. A. Ellissen, *Der Senat im öström. Reiche*, 1881, 33; but I could not verify his incomplete quotation (p. 26, vv. 431 ff.). Cf. Ammianus xxi. 16. 2, and, on him, Seeck, op. cit. iv. 395 (on p. 34 l. 25).

[7] Seeck, op. cit. iv. 34 ff.

[8] Cf. my preliminary sketch in *Die Kontorniaten*, 1943, 50 ff.

Rome. But we should land ourselves in perplexities if we judged Constantius in this matter simply and solely by expressions in literature: they give such contradictory reports of him.

Aurelius Victor, for example, served up the carefully staged appearance of the Emperor before the two armies, which led to the abdication of Vetranio as the result of Constantius' enchanting and irresistible eloquence, as a triumph to be compared to the political victories of the famous orators of the forum of the free Republic.[1] Themistius, too, depicts in Constantius the great patron of the literary and rhetorical culture of the age,[2] who restores that philosophy that was steadily vanishing from human circles, and whom he praises in rapturous tones in the company of Plato as the embodiment of the philosopher-king.[3] But quite different are the expressions of Libanius, the great orator of Antioch, the antagonist of Themistius:

'Constantius II visited the sophistic culture with as much discredit as he did its natural concomitant, the pagan religion (lxii. 8), refusing to have any dealings whatsoever with its practitioners. He would not invite any of the sophists to the palace, but welcomed in their stead a crowd of eunuchs (lxii. 9), more numerous than the flies that swarm around shepherds in the spring (xviii. 130), to say nothing of hundreds of cooks, barbers (cf. Ammianus xxii. 4. 9) wine-pourers, and caterers' satellites who would admit only the despised clerics and shorthand-writers to the Emperor's presence (cf. lxii. 10 and 51). While sons of cooks and fullers exulted in unaccustomed wealth and dignity, no rhetor could secure an office except by cajoling these base courtiers. So there was no cause for remark that the youths in school grew convinced that theirs was a futile grind, which would in no way enhance their prospects after graduation, or that their fathers were also disheartened when they saw that students at Athens itself, after leaving the Lyceum with all its Aristotelian learning, had no career open to them better than that of a secret investigator (*agens in rebus*) (lxii. 11–14). He could, however,

---

[1] Victor, *Caes.* 42. 1–4: 'quae gloria post natum imperium soli processit eloquio clementiaque. nam cum magna parte utrimque exercitus convenissent, habita ad speciem iudicii contione, quod fere vix aut multo sanguine obtinendum erat, eloquentia patravit. quae res satis edocuit non modo domi, verum militiae quoque dicendi copiam praestare.' Cf. *Epit. de Caes.* 42. 18.

[2] Themist. *or.* 3, p. 54. 21 ff. Dind., *or.* 4, p. 65. 8 ff. Dind.

[3] Themist. *or.* 3, p. 56. 3 ff.; *or.* 4, pp. 73. 11 ff., 31 ff., 74. 20 ff., &c. See also above, pp. 108 f.

name five of his students who had served successfully as administrators (54–62).'[1]

In the Roman East, the regular and proper sphere of Constantius, it was the grammarians, rhetoricians, and philosophers who fought against the peasants and barbarians, in the first place, not the great noble landowners; here the reaction was not inspired by the defence of their political traditions and class interests, but at most by the mere struggle to exist of those who lived on this culture. Though the Church, too, from the point of view of education was thrown back on the teaching of the world of classical thought, as well as on rhetoric and grammar, it was tending to crush the cultural movement that rested on tradition, and so was at the same time pagan; but Christianity utterly failed as yet to break the conception that the classical culture was the one corner-stone of the rule of the Emperor.

Themistius' testimony to the activity of Constantius in patronizing literature loses much of its value when we find him singing the same praises of Jovian at the beginning of his reign—of Jovian who had no time for the development of any cultural policy whatsoever. His early death was a reason, but not the only one. Themistius even strikes very strange new notes: culture till now has been neglected—the new Emperor has restored it to its ancient rights—and all this after that great reaction in favour of culture which he himself has been extolling under Constantius and Julian![2] We see how anxious the men of letters must be to inspire the right kind of attitude in the holders of power—the speeches of Themistius are, from this point of view, lessons indeed—but the men for whom the lessons were meant had already learned them.

The situation was not changed immediately, even under the reigns of the two Pannonian brothers. Valens, who was not as talented or energetic as his brother, may have been lazy about learning, for he never attained the same grade of culture as his

[1] R. A. Pack, *Studies in Libanius and Antiochene Society under Theodosius*, Diss., Michigan, 1935, 5.

[2] Themist. *or.* 5, pp. 75 ff. Dind., especially 75, ll. 18 ff.: ὅτι φιλοσοφίαν οὐ πάνυ παρὰ τοῖς πολλοῖς εὐπραγοῦσαν κατὰ τὸν παρόντα χρόνον ἐπανάγεις αὖθις εἰς τὰ βασίλεια, κτλ.

elder brother. If Ammianus seizes every opportunity to depict his lack of polish, that is due in part to the senatorial reaction, in part to the bitterness of a cultured man, coming from a Greek and pagan milieu, towards the highest Christian child of fortune, from whom he has nothing to expect.[1] The old resentment of the cultured East against the hard-handed Pannonian Emperors breaks out when the rebel Procopius calls Valens a 'dissolute' Pannonian,[2] when he is mocked from the walls of Chalcedon as a *sabaiarius*, a drinker of the wretched barley-wine of Pannonia,[3] or when Libanius, in connexion with the execution following the charges of magic connected with Theodorus, calls him simply, in disdain, the 'Pannonian Emperor'.[4]

It is interesting to observe how Themistius actually casts his 'rusticity' in the teeth of the Emperor—under a show of good-will and reverence, it is true, in order to lead him to a better estimation of culture. We seem to feel something of the moral courage of the Christian preacher of the Word when he describes the role of Valens like Victor in his characterization of the Lords of the Tetrarchy:[5] 'ruris ac militiae miseriis imbuti satis optimi rei publicae fuere'—'brought up to land work and to the miseries of the soldier's life they were none the less very good for the State'[6]—but only declares the more emphatically that the support of philosophy is the duty of every good Emperor and that it is only tyrants who persecute the philosophers.[7]

Themistius, in his kindly admonitions to Valens, is aiming

[1] Ammianus xxix. 1. 11: 'Valentem, subrusticum hominem'; xxx. 4. 2: 'subagreste ingenium, nullis vetustatis lectionibus expolitum'; xxxi. 14. 5: 'subagrestis ingenii, nec bellicis, nec liberalibus studiis eruditus'; xxvi. 10. 2 on Serenianus: 'incultis moribus homo . . . Valentique ob similitudinem morum, et genitalis patriae vicinitatem acceptus'; xxvii. 5. 8: 'imperator rudis'; xxix. 2. 18, quoted below; xxxi. 14. 8: 'ut erat inconsummatus et rudis'.

[2] Ibid. xxvi. 7. 16: 'Pannonius degener'.

[3] Ibid. 8. 2.

[4] Libanius, *or*. xlvi. 30 (3, p. 394 Foerster): ὁ Παίων βασιλεύς.

[5] Victor, *Caes*. 39. 26.

[6] See Note 56, p. 144.

[7] Themist. *or*. 1. 6, pp. 85 ff. Dind.

but now, for a long time, he wavered between the two poles. Only in A.D. 394 did he finally make a break with the ideas of the Roman 'tradition of the ancestors' and thus determine the way that his successors must take. It can still happen that Themistius,[1] urging him, in spite of his slight education, to patronize culture, describes him as 'the philosopher in the purple'.[2] Certainly, in the dedication of the *Annals* of Nicomachus Flavianus[3] the praises of his high culture were sung at length.

Other courtiers and panegyrists, of course, followed Themistius in singing the praises of the high level of culture of their epoch and of the acts in its defence due to the Emperors of the fifth century; but these are no more than flowers of speech, without any real significance.

This, then, was the framework within which the whole of the reaction against Valentinian was set. Let us now see briefly how the Pannonian soldier behaved towards culture.

The hostile pagan tradition, represented by Zosimus, denies him any kind of culture,[4] and, when Symmachus, agitating against Maximinus, mocks his *externi mores*, his un-Roman ways, he is undoubtedly including Valentinian in the company of the barbarians.[5] Ammianus tauntingly calls him 'rustic',[6]

---

[1] The author of the *Epitome de Caesaribus*, composed in his reign or in that of his son, can only veil his inferior education with the pretence that he has an interest in history: 48. 11: 'litteris, si nimium perfectos contemplemur, mediocriter doctus; sagax plane multumque diligens ad noscenda maiorum gesta'. This interest is stressed by the Emperor himself: cf. his letter to Ausonius (Auson. *opusc.* ed. Peiper, p. 3).

[2] Themist. *or.* 34, p. 453. 4 ff. Dind.: φιλόσοφος ἐν ἁλουργίδι; cf. also p. 450. 10 ff.

[3] Dessau, *I.L.S.* 2948. Cf. W. Hartke, *Geschichte und Politik im spätantiken Rom* (*Klio*, Beih. xlv), 1940, 36. 143 f., 159, n. 3; E. A. Thompson, op. cit. 110.

[4] Zosimus iii. 36. 2: πολέμων δὲ μετασχὼν οὐκ ὀλίγων παιδεύσεως οὐδεμιᾶς μετεσχήκε.   [5] See above, pp. 69 f.

[6] Ammianus xxix. 3. 6: 'subagrestis'. The comment of Seeck (*Gesch. d. Unt. d. ant. Welt*, v. 422, on p. 3. 1. 8) deserves attention. Ammianus xxvi. 1. 4 says of Equitius that his candidature was given up, 'cum potiorum auctoritate displicuisset ut asper et subagrestis'. The same objection could not, then, well be made against Valentinian, who was preferred to him.

but in another place he talks, as we shall see, in quite another tone about him.[1]

It is a fact that Valentinian had a good knowledge of Greek, but no Greek education.[2] On the other hand, his intensive education in Latin is attested, and the authority on which Ammianus and the author of the *Epitome de Caesaribus* both draw[3] describes him as a sensitive and refined man of education. This man of fresh spirit and remarkable memory could talk in magnificent phrases, although he did not care to talk much; his writings were composed in the artificial style then prevalent; he could paint with a true sense for art and could model statues; he could construct original weapons, he took a delight in the joys of a life of culture and also in fine, but not over-luxurious, banquets; his contemporaries compared him to Hadrian. Consistent with this picture are the other minor traits that we know of him. He apparently knew his Virgil by heart, for he could venture to compete with Ausonius in mixing and twisting the expressions of the great heroic epic to compose a frivolous 'Marriage Cento'.[4] He never for one moment denied[5] that the higher culture was an indispensable

[1] H. Schiller, *Gesch. d. r. Kaiser*, ii, 1887, 365, and O. Seeck, op. cit. 422 on p. 2, l. 34 suppose that he knew no Greek; but W. Heering, *Kaiser Valentinian*, i, 1927, 65 (and E. Stein, *Gesch. d. spätrömischen Reiches*, i, 1928, 267) have refuted them, by quoting Ammianus (xxx. 5. 9), where the Emperor deals with the envoys of the Epirotes in Greek.

[2] Themist. *or.* 9, p. 150. 26 ff. (Dind.) says to Valentinian II: οὐδὲ γὰρ τὸν πατέρα τὸν σὸν τὸ μὴ τοῖς ῥήμασιν ἀττικίζειν διεκώλυσε πρᾳότερον νομισθῆναι τῶν πώποτε αὐτοκρατόρων κτλ.

[3] Ammianus xxx. 9. 4: 'scribens decore, venusteque pingens et fingens et novorum inventor armorum: memoria sermoneque incitato quidem sed raro, facundiae proximo vigens, amator munditiarum, laetusque non profusis epulis sed excultis'; *Epit. de Caes.* 45. 5–6: 'hic Valentinianus fuit vultu decens, sollers ingenio, animo gravis, sermone cultissimus, quamquam esset ad loquendum parcus...; et in his, quae memoraturus sum, Hadriano proximus: pingere venustissime, meminisse, nova arma meditari, fingere cera seu limo simulacra, prudenter uti locis, temporibus, sermone'.

[4] Ausonius, *Cento nuptialis* 1. Cf. also Seeck, *Gesch. d. Unt. d. ant. Welt*, v. 15.

[5] Ammianus puts the following words into his mouth, as he presents his son to the army, before proclaiming him Emperor: 'ut enim mihi videri solet mores eius et adpetitus, licet nondum maturos, saepe pensanti: ineunte adulescentia, quoniam humanitate et studiis disciplinarum sollertium est expolitus, librabit suffragiis puris merita recte secusve factorum' (xxvii. 6. 9).

part of Empire, and he let his son be educated by the famous poet of the age, Ausonius.[1]

We must not, of course, expect of him that he should place the fostering of the ancient culture in the centre of his home policy; that would have been equivalent to a continuation of the heathen reaction of Julian, and his ideas were at least as far removed from his as from those of Constantius, who was almost a Caesar-Pope. He stood above both sides and, while he looked out far beyond them, his eyes were held by the dark clouds gathering on the frontiers. At home he was concerned to redeem the ruin of morals with an iron hand and to bring in a sound social and financial policy in order that the great Empire might be made ready to face the storms that were fast coming up from abroad.

And now at last for a short retrospect. The attitude of the late historians, which stigmatizes the last phase of the rule of the Pannonian Emperors as a reign of terror conducted by barbarians against culture, is the propaganda of prejudiced partisans. In Zosimus we hear the voice of the 'Hellene', the pagan man of culture of the East, in whose eyes the Christian is always the representative of backward ignorance; the Latin historians utter their declamations in the name of the claims of the Senate and seek in the slogans of the higher culture a title-deed to use against them.

It is, alas, true that Valentinian was not raised by his education to the heights of the spirit of classical Greek, that he had no magic wand in his pocket to enable him to conjure back ancient culture, withering and in decay, to a new prime. But what of the far more thorough education of Julian? It tended, characteristically enough, to develop into a religious and mystical emotionalism, and if it had enjoyed a longer duration, it would not so much have revived the Greek and Roman method of inductive thought as rather have taken the abstract line of the age and developed pagan intolerance to the pitch of pitiful oppression. Could it have produced a new birth? I cannot believe it.

The last great Pannonian Emperor, for all that his historical mission lay in other fields, had still a sufficiently wide outlook

[1] Seeck, op. cit. v. 441 on p. 41, l. 8.

and a sufficiently adequate education not to accelerate the decline of culture. On the contrary, his measured policy in religion did not permit the wild destruction of the monuments of ancient art, which, from the later years of Constantine to Julian and again after his death, by demolition of the pagan temples and statues and by the ruin or neglect of the literary monuments of the ancient spirit, had caused such inconceivable damage to *humanitas*.

This theme we shall have soon to treat in greater detail.

APPENDIX

THE EMPEROR AFTER THE SENATE'S HEART IN THE *HISTORIA AUGUSTA*

THE political aspirations of the Roman Senate at the very end of the fourth century A.D. are sharply mirrored in the so-called *Historia Augusta* (cf. last monograph on it: J. Straub, *Studien zur Historia Augusta*, Diss. Bernenses, ser. i. 4, 1951). The set forms which carefully recorded the attitude of every Emperor towards the *patres* were of course already to be found in the sources used by the author of this compilation. It is evident, too, that in the earlier writers such observations corresponded to the facts, though the manner in which the facts are described already betrays the tendency. Thus Cassius Dio records that Titus, the good Emperor, does not put to death any senator (lxvi. 19. 1), only the bad Domitian (lxvii. 2. 4); that after Domitian, Nerva and Trajan take the oath not to kill any man of senatorial rank (lxviii. 2. 3; 5. 2); that Marcus (lxxi. 28. 2) and Pertinax (lxxii. 8. 5) generously abstain from shedding the blood of a noble, whereas the malicious Septimius Severus does not keep his oath (lxxiv. 2. 1) promising to refrain from such murders; that Macrinus solemnly declared, as being a senator himself, he cannot kill such men (lxxviii. 21. 3), &c.

But in the *Historia Augusta* the true facts are superseded by mendacious statements to extol the overwhelming authority of the *patres*. As only the original wording can give a clear idea of the zeal of the author to stress this tendency, we give here a series of characteristic quotations. *Vita Hadr.* 7. 4: 'in senatu excusatis quae facta erant, iuravit se numquam senatorem nisi ex senatus sententia puniturum'. Ibid. 8. 7 ff.: 'senatus fastigium in tantum extulit . . .; exsecratus est denique principes, qui minus senatoribus detulissent'. *Vita Pii* 6. 5: 'senatui tantum detulit imperator, quantum, cum privatus esset, deferri sibi ab alio principe optavit'. *Vita Marci* 10. 2: 'neque quisquam principum amplius senatui detulit'. Ibid. 25. 6: 'simul petit, ne qui senator tempore principatus sui occideretur, ne eius pollueretur imperium'; cf. 26. 13, 29. 4. *Vita Avid. Cass.* 8. 7, 12. 4: 'nemo senatorum puniatur, nullius fundatur viri nobilis sanguis'. *Vita Commodi* 3. 9: 'in senatus odium ita venit, ut et ipse crudeliter in tanti ordinis perniciem saeviret fieretque e contempto crudelis'; 5. 12: 'multique senatores sine iudicio interempti'. *Vita Pertin.* 13. 2: 'fuit in curia honorificentissimus, ita ut senatum faventem adoraret et quasi praefectus urbi cum omnibus sermonem participaret'. *Vita Severi* 7. 5: 'fieri etiam senatus consultum coegit, ne liceret imperatori inconsulto senatu occidere senatorem'; 12. 9 ff.: 'post hoc de sua clementia disseruit, cum crudelissimus fuerit, et senatores infra scriptos occiderit. . . . horum igitur tantorum ac tam inlustrium virorum . . . interfector. . . '. *Vita Alex.* 52. 2: 'ἀναίματον imperium eius, cum fuerit durus et tetricus, idcirco vocatum est, quod senatorem nullum occiderit, ut Herodianus Graecus scriptor refert in libris temporum suorum'. *Maximini duo* 9. 6: 'nobilem circa se neminem passus est'. *Vita Aureliani* 21. 5–6: 'incivilius denique usus imperio, vir alias optimus, . . . interfecti sunt enim nonnulli etiam nobiles senatores, cum his leve quiddam et quod contemni a mitiore principe potuisset vel unus vel levis testis obiceret'. *Vita Tac.* 9. 1: 'ita mihi liceat p.c.', says the Emperor, 'sic imperium regere, ut a vobis me constet electum, ut ego cuncta ex vestra facere sententia et potestate decrevi. vestrum est igitur ea iubere atque sancire, quae digna vobis, digna modesto exercitu, digna populo Romano esse videantur'; 9. 6 (he is happy that the Senate rejected a proposition of his!): 'multum laetatus senatus libertate'. Ibid. 12. 1–2: 'nec tacendum est et frequenter intimandum tantam senatus laetitiam fuisse, quod eligendi principis cura ad ordinem amplissimum revertisset, ut et supplicationes decernerentur, et hecatombe permitteretur, singuli denique senatores ad suos scriberent nec ad suos tantum sed etiam ad externos, mitterentur praeterea litterae ad provincias: scirent omnes socii omnesque nationes in antiquum statum redisse rem p., ac senatum principes legere, immo ipsum senatum principem factum, leges a senatu petendas, reges barbaros senatui supplicaturos, pacem ac bella senatu auctore tractanda. ne quid denique deesset cognitioni, plerasque huiusmodi epistulas in fine libri posui et cum cupiditate et sine fastidio, ut aestimo, perlegendas.' Ibid. 4. 3: 'princeps senatus recte Augustus creatur, primae sententiae vir recte imperator creatur'. Ibid. 15. 2 (a forged prophecy, after the statement that an Emperor of the lineage of Tacitus will conquer the world, but) 'postea tamen senatui reddat imperium et antiquis legibus vivat'. *Vita Probi* 11. 2: 'oratio Probi prima ad senatum: "recte atque ordine, p.c., proximo superiore anno factum est, ut, vestra clementia orbi terrarum principem daret, et quidem de vobis, qui et estis mundi principes et semper fuistis et in vestris posteris eritis"'. Ibid. 13. 1: 'permisit patribus, ut ex magnorum iudicum appellationibus ipsi cognoscerent, proconsules crearent, legatos ex consulibus darent, ius praetorium praesidibus darent, leges, quas Probus ederet, senatus consultis propriis consecrarent' (all pure invention).

All this was produced for the consumption of the nobility in the years after the battle on the Frigidus, when the political chances of the Senate were gone for ever; but the dreams of the glorious past were still dreamed—not without afterthoughts on their realization. How much more hopeful such a revival of the senatorial power may have looked under Valentinian! And as events demonstrated, their secret aspirations were not smaller.

NOTES

1 (p. 3). Cf., for example, W. Ensslin, *Zur Geschichtsschreibung und Welt-anschauung des Ammianus Marcellinus*, 1923, 87 ff.; W. Hartke, 'Geschichte und Politik im spätantiken Rom' (*Klio*, Beiheft lii, 1940), 74 ff. If numerous earlier studies have been all too ready to suspect the copying by Ammianus of some definite literary source, the latest monograph on his work—I mean the able and valuable study of E. A. Thompson, *The Historical Work of Ammianus Marcellinus*, 1947, 21 ff.—would deny almost completely the use of single special sources. But he admits (p. 39) the possible use of the *Annals* of Nicomachus Flavianus for the sections on the history of Rome, and it cannot reasonably be doubted that Ammianus in his account of the events in the Eternal City followed a written report.

2 (p. 9). L. R. Dean, *A Study of Cognomina of Soldiers in the Roman Legions*, Diss. Princeton, 1916; A. Nagl, *RE*. vii A. 2097, 2159. Cf. also *C.I.L.* iii, Index. The question might be raised whether Valentinian inherited the name of Flavius from his predecessors or adopted it in an attempt to secure the popularity of the dynasty of Constantine, as did Odovakar later. Septimius Severus, at an earlier date, had linked his dynasty to that of his popular predecessors, and had named his elder son M. Aurelius Antoninus, falsifying his own descent. The trait is not peculiar to Valentinian, then; but the expression 'secundum parentis nostri Constantini divale praeceptum' (*Cod. Th.* xiv. 3. 12) points in this direction. And Marius Victorinus, *De trinitate* 2, calls Constantine *the father* of Valentinian! Cf. also the remarks of Gothofredus on the law just quoted. The marriage of his son with the posthumous daughter of Constantius II shows that Valentinian was eager to connect his house with the preceding dynasty.

3 (p. 11). Seeck, *Gesch. d. Unt. d. ant. Welt*, v. 1, can only be moved by prejudice and malice when he writes: 'But once again envy and dislike prevented any general who had given proof of his worth from being considered. After some hesitation they agreed, on the advice of Salutius, on a man, who . . . was as insignificant as Jovian had been before his elevation.' But how could envy and dislike play a part, when the judgement of the wise old Salutius was decisive? And if they had been looking for an insignificant aspirant, they could have found immediately any number of them and need not have chosen the unsuspecting and absent Valentinian.

4 (p. 12). Symm. *or*. i. 8 (p. 320, Seeck): 'excesserat divus Iovianus e terris ac se improviso fine subtraxerat. maestum omnium repente iustitium, nec ulla, ut adsolet, murmura factionum. cessabat ambitus, quia dignus extabat. ecquis miratur non ilico in te conversa suffragia? nulla causa properandi est, ubi non suspecta dilatio, et saepe minuit boni facti laudem, quisquis ei obesse existimat tarditatem. ergo servatus es iudicio multitudinis, nequis te mussitaret praeiudicium captasse paucorum. nihil circa honorem tuum sibi adsumit eventus; ab iis imperator electus es, qui deliberarunt'; Ammianus xxvi. 1. 5: 'Valentinianus, nulla discordante sententia, numinis adspiratione caelestis electus est . . .; et quia nullo renitente hoc e re publica videbatur, missi sunt

qui eum venire ocius admonerent, diebusque decem nullus imperii tenuit gubernacula'. The part of the army was limited to the simple acclamation; ibid. 2. 1 ff.

5 (p. 20). Eutropius *Brev.* 10. 1. 2 (on the Emperor Constantius Chlorus): 'vir egregius et praestantissimae civilitatis, divitiis provincialium ac privatorum studens, fisci commoda non admodum affectans, dicensque melius publicas opes a privatis haberi, quam intra unum claustrum reservari', &c. The comment on the liberality or stinginess of every Emperor is never missing in any of the late Roman historical compendia. I would like to quote some characteristic statements of the *Historia Augusta*. *Vita Hadr.* 15. 1: 'amicos ditavit et quidem non petentes, cum petentibus nil negaret'; *Vita Marci* 3. 9, *Vita Sev.* 7. 9: 'amicorum dehinc aes alienum dissolvit'; *Vita Aurel.* 45. 3: 'amicos suos honeste ditavit, et modice, ut miserias paupertatis effugerent et divitiarum invidiam patrimonii moderatione vitarent', &c.

6 (p. 26). Ammianus xxx. 8. 8–9: 'aviditas plus habendi, sine honesti pravique differentia, et indagandi quaestus varios per alienae vitae naufragia exundavit in hoc principe flagrantius aduliscens. quam equidem praetendentes imperatorem Aurelianum purgare temptant, id affirmando quod, ut ille post Gallienum et lamentabilis rei publicae casus, exinanito aerario, torrentis ritu ferebatur in divites, ita hic quoque post procinctus Parthici clades, magnitudine indigens impensarum, ut militi supplementa suppeterent et stipendium, crudelitati cupiditatem opes nimias congerendi miscebat, dissimulans scire quod sunt aliqua quae fieri non oportet, etiam si licet, Themistoclis illius verecundi dissimilis, qui cum post pugnam agminaque deleta Persarum, licenter obambulans, armillas aureas vidisset humi proiectas et torquem, "tolle", inquit, "haec", ad comitem quendam prope adstantem versus, "quia Themistocles non es", quodlibet spernens in duce magnanimo lucrum . . . huius exempla continentiae similia plurima in Romanis exuberant ducibus: quibus omissis, quoniam non sunt perfectae virtutis indicia—nec enim aliena non rapere laudis est—unum ex multis constans innocentiae vulgi veteris specimen ponam. cum proscriptorum locupletes domus diripiendas Romanae plebei Marius dedisset et Cinna, ita vulgi rudes animi sed humana soliti respectare, alienis laboribus pepercerunt, ut nullus egens reperiretur aut infimus, qui de civili luctu fructum contrectare pateretur sibi concessum.'

7 (p. 26). Ammianus xxviii. 1. 20: one point in the accusation against a Roman aristocrat, Hymetius, charged with high treason ,was that at the end of a letter addressed to a *haruspex* 'quaedam invectiva legebantur in principem ut avarum et truculentum'. The *Epit. de Caes.*, that appeared about the time of Theodosius, mentions (45. 5–6), after a record of his outstanding qualities, that he was 'severus, vehemens, infectus vitiis maximeque avaritiae cuius [punitor] ipse fuit acer'. Similar charges were brought against Valens and for the same reasons: cf. Ammianus xxvi. 6. 6, xxix. 1. 19, 21, 43, xxxi. 14. 5.

8 (p. 34). Ammianus xxvii. 3. 10 (on the prefect of the City, Lampadius): 'aedificia erigere exordiens nova, vel vetusta quaedam instaurans, non ex titulis solitis, parari iubebat impensas, sed si ferrum quaerebatur, aut

plumbum, aut aes aut quicquam simile, apparitores inmittebantur, qui velut ementes diversas raperent species, nulla pretia persolvendo, unde accensorum iracundiam pauperum, damna deflentium crebra, aegre potuit celeri vitare digressu'. Themistius in A.D. 369 seems to be pointing to the recent abuses of the aristocratic governors when he writes (*or.* 8, p. 137. 29 ff. Dind.): οὐδὲν γὰρ τῷ πάσχοντι κακῶς τὸν Σκύθην ἢ 'Ρωμαῖον εἶναι τὸν ἀδικοῦντα, ἀλλ' ὑφ' ὅτουπερ ἂν πάσχῃ κακῶς, τοῦτον εἶναι τὸν πολέμιον οἴεται. καὶ πολλοὶ τῶν εὐπατρι- δῶν τὰ σκῆπτρα ἐκ τριγονίας δ'αδεξάμενοι ποθεινοὺς ἐποίησαν τοὺς βαρβάρους τοῖς ὑπηκόοις. ἀλλά, οὐ νῦν, ἀλλ' ἀκολουθεῖ τῇ φύσει τοῦ γένους τό τε οἰκεῖον καὶ τὸ ἀλλότριον. οἱ μὲν ἀγαπῶσιν, οἱ δὲ πεφρίκασιν.

9 (p. 39). Ammianus xxix. 5. 24: 'quod salutaris rigor vincit inanem speciem clementiae'. Similarly, only in a roundabout way, he ventures to criticize the bloody severity with which he proceeded against the rebel soldiers in Africa, xxix. 5. 22–3: 'eos, qui inter Constantianos merebant, prisco more militibus dedidit occidendos, Sagittariorum vero primoribus manus incidit, residuos supplicio capitali multavit, ad aemulationem Curionis, acerrimi illius ducis, qui Dardanorum ferociam, in modum Lernaeae serpentis aliquotiens renascentem, hoc genere poenarum extinxit. sed obtrectatores malevoli vetus factum laudantes, hoc ut dirum vituperant et asperrimum, Dardanos hostes memorantes internicivos, et iuste quae sustinuere perpessos, hos vero subsignanos milites debuisse lenius corrigi, ad unum prolapsos errorem. quos nescientes fortasse admonemus . . .' &c. Even more significant is 24, where he excuses his bloody executions. On the military achievements of Theodosius the Elder cf. now A. Piganiol, *L'Empire chrétien*, 1947, 179 ff.

10 (p. 42). Ammianus xxvii. 7. 6–7: 'dein cum in negotio Maxentii cuiusdam Pannonii, ob exsecutionem a iudice recte maturari praeceptam, trium oppi- dorum ordines mactari iussisset, interpellavit Eupraxius, tunc quaestor, et, "parcius" inquit, "agito, piissime principum: hos enim, quos interfici tamquam noxios iubes, ut martyras, (id est divinitati acceptos) colit religio Christiana". cuius salutarem fiduciam praefectus imitatus Florentius, cum in re quadam venia digna audisset, eum percitum ira, iussisse itidem ternos per ordines urbium interfici plurimarum. "et quid agitur?" ait, "si oppidum aliquod curialis non haberet tantos? inter reliqua id quoque suspendi debet, ut cum habuerit occidantur".' The words of the quaestor no doubt did not run quite like this, nor can the furious threat be authentic. It might have been like the curse, pronounced in sudden excitement, recorded in ibid. 8: 'itemque aliud audiebatur horrendum, quod ubi debitorum aliquem egestate obstri- ctum, nihil posse reddere discebat, interfici debere pronuntiabat'. A similar case is that described in xxx. 5. 19, where the writer takes pleasure in describ- ing a furious threat which leaves an impression of genuine horror but which was never actually carried out: 'progressus deinde matutinus, contractiore vultu subtristis, cum eum oblatus non susciperet equus, anteriores pedes praeter morem erigens in sublime, innata feritate concitus, ut erat inmanis, dexteram stratoris militis iussit abscidi, quae eum insilientem iumento fulserat consuete: perissetque cruciabiliter innocens iuvenis, ni tribunus stabuli Cerealis dirum nefas cum sui periculo distulisset'.

11 (p. 42). Ammianus xxix. 3. 9: 'illud tamen nec praeteriri est aequum nec sileri, quod cum duas haberet ursas saevas hominum ambestrices, Micam auream et Innocentiam, cultu ita curabat enixo, ut earum caveas prope cubiculum suum locaret, custodesque adderet fidos, visuros sollicite, ne quo casu ferarum deleretur luctificus calor. Innocentiam denique, post multas quas eius laniatu cadaverum viderat sepulturas, ut bene meritam in silvas abire dimisit innoxiam, exoptans similes edituram.' It is possible that Valentinian kept two bears and that they were no pet lambs. The passion of the Empire for fights between wild beasts and men in the arena might even make us believe that these wild beasts were exhibited there. But that this believer in Christ, with his stern personal discipline, really had men mangled by the dozen for his amusement contradicts all the reliable evidence that we have of his character. We must the more readily reject this story because it is apparently no more than an ordinary traveller's tale, one of those which, on other occasions, too, were spread about Emperors who were branded as tyrants; compare what Lactantius tells us about the hated Galerius (*De mortibus persecutorum* 21. 5–6): 'quid lusorium vel delicias eius referam? habebat ursos ferociae ac magnitudinis suae simillimos, quos toto imperii sui tempore elegerat. quotiens delectari libuerat, horum aliquem adferri nominatim iubebat. his homines non plane comedendi, sed obsorbendi obiectabantur: quorum artus cum dissiparentur, ridebat suavissime; nec unquam sine humano cruore cenabat'. We must, however, feel surprised when the distinguished Seeck (*Gesch. d. Unt. d. ant. Welt*, v. 9), adapting himself to the tone of Ammianus, accepts this story as true; other scholars have followed him (Heering, *Kaiser Valentinianus*, i, 1927, 66 ff.).

12 (p. 42). We will just quote a few characteristic cases: Ammianus xxx. 8. 13 does not emphasize the really vital point that Valentinian reposed an exaggerated confidence in those whom he, out of his best conviction, had chosen out for the highest posts ('iudices numquam consulto malignos elegit, sed si semel promotos agere didicisset inmaniter, Lycurgos invenisse praedicabat et Cassios, columina iustitiae prisca'), but represents his instructions to proceed strictly as brutal lust of destruction ('scribensque hortabatur adsidue, ut noxas vel leves acerbius vindicarent'). If he was deaf to complaints against his confidants, he ascribes it to his inhumanity ('nec adflictis . . . erat ullum in principis benignitate perfugium'). Valentinian was compelled, in view of the crushing burdens of the Persian campaign, to tighten up the collection of taxes: 'post procinctus Parthici clades, magnitudine indigens inpensarum, ut militi supplementa suppeterent et stipendium' (xxx. 8. 8); Ammianus' interpretation is: 'crudelitati cupiditatem opes nimias congerendi miscebat'. Quite incredible for Valentinian is the following charge (xxx. 8. 10): 'invidia . . . medullitus urebatur . . ., memorabat adsidue, livorem severitatis rectae potestatis esse individuam sociam'. When the *magister officiorum*, Remigius, succeeded in mastering the anger of his lord by adroitly turning the conversation towards the barbarians who were harassing the frontiers of the Empire (xxx. 8. 12), that was no mark of cowardice, but proof of that serious concern which well beseemed an Emperor. We shall see later that such a concern filled

Valentinian's whole being. When the Alamanni had butchered a Roman detachment which had been building a fort in their territory, the Emperor merely dismissed the confidential agent whom he had entrusted to survey the operation (xxviii. 2. 9); our author describes this dismissal as *scaevum arbitrium*—a serious exaggeration—apart from the question whether the man in question, the *notarius* Syagrius, was guilty or not.

13 (p. 43). Ammianus xxx. 8. 2: 'adsimulavit non nunquam clementiae speciem, cum esset in acerbitatem naturae calore propensior'; xxii. 7. 4: 'et quamquam Valentinianus, homo propalam ferus, inter imperitandi exordia, ut asperitatis opinionem molliret, impetus truces retinere non numquam in potestate animi nitebatur, serpens tamen vitium et dilatum, licentius erupit ad perniciem plurimorum, quod auxit ira acerbius effervescens'. (Here the rhetorical scheme of the gradual deterioration of the tyrant may have played its part.) xxix. 3. 2: 'trux suopte ingenio Valentinianus (becoming more and more cruel at the instigation of his confidant, Maximinus) ... per asperos actus velut aestu quodam fluctuum ferebatur et procellarum, adeo ut irascentis saepe vox et vultus et incessus mutaretur et color'. The heathen Zosimus, who cannot endure him because he is a Christian and an opponent of Julian, calls him both cruel and passionate (iv. 1. 1).

14 (p. 43). Ammianus (xxx. 8. 2) describes this in him as hypocrisy: 'adsimulavit non numquam clementiae speciem', and goes on to reproach him with his violent nature, 'oblitus ... quod regenti imperium, omnia nimia ... sunt evitanda', and records the 'exempla ... maiorum ... peregrina atque interna humanitatis et pietatis' (ibid. 4–7) which should have served him as model; but, in fact, palpable proofs of his self-control survive. On another occasion Ammianus (xxvii. 7. 4) does admit that at the beginning of his reign he disciplined himself better: 'inter imperitandi exordia, ut asperitatis opinionem molliret, impetus truces retinere non numquam in potestate animi nitebatur'. His own expressions, when he speaks of his *moderatio, mansuetudo*, and *indulgentia* (O. Seeck, *Gesch. d. Unt. d. ant. Welt*, v, pp. 10 ff.) are no empty phrases, then (cf. above, p. 55).

15 (p. 44). We have already seen how Remigius was able to disarm his wrath by pointing to the troublesome movements of the barbarians (Ammianus xxx. 8. 12). The *quaestor sacri palatii*, Eupraxius, brings him to his senses when he is purposing to exterminate the decurions of three cities (Ammianus xxvii. 7. 6); in a similar case, he is at once pacified by the warning of the *praefectus praetorio*, Florentius (xxvii. 7. 7). Ammianus is not unjust when, just after describing these cases, he writes (xxvii. 7. 9): 'haec autem et similia licenter ideo altiore fastu quidam principes agunt, quod amicis emendandi secus cogitata vel gesta copiam negant ...'. On other occasions he accepts the appeal of the *tribunus stabuli*, Cerealis (Ammianus xxx. 5. 19), and there is no doubt that such an attitude was in general characteristic of him. A similar example is given by Themistius (*or.* 7, pp. 101 ff. Dind.) of Valens, where he informs the Emperor of the requirements of the higher culture, in the course of begging mercy for those compromised in the revolt of Procopius.

16 (p. 45). Ammianus xxx. 8. 13: 'iudices numquam consulto malignos elegit'; Zonaras xiii. 15. 4–6 (p. 73 Buettner-Wobst): *οὗτος καὶ τὴν ἰσχὺν γενναιότατος καὶ τὴν γνώμην ἦν δικαιότατος*; Cedrenus, p. 541. 7 Bonn: *οὐ καὶ τὸ αὐστηρὸν διὰ τὸ δίκαιον ἐπηνεῖτο καὶ ἐθαυμάζετο· οὐ γὰρ ἄνευ λόγου τὸ αὐστηρὸν ἐκέκτητο, ἀλλ' ἀεὶ τῷ δικαίῳ τὰ πρῶτα παρεῖχεν, ὑπ' οὐδενὸς ἐκ τούτου περιτρεπόμενος, οὐδὲ μετατιθέμενος ἐξ ὧν ἅπαξ ἐβουλεύσατο.* Ausonius, *Grat. act.* 6: 'alta bonitas, temperata severitas'; *Narratio de imp. domus Valent. et Theodos.* = *Mon. Germ. Hist., auct. ant.* ix, p. 629: 'severus et strenuus imperator'; Ioh. Antioch. frg. 182 (*F.H.G.* iv. 607 = *Exc. de virt.* ed. A. G. Roos, p. 201, no. 65); Theodoret, *H.E.* iv. 6. 1; Eunap. *Hist.* frg. 53 (*F.H.G.* iv. 37).

17 (p. 46). This, I think, is how we should understand the passage in Ammianus (xxix. 3. 4): 'praepositum fabricae oblato thorace polito faberrime, praemiumque ideo exspectantem, ea re praecepit occidi . . . quod pondus paulo minus habuit species ferrea, quam ille firmarat'. I am not sure whether our author, himself a soldier, is deliberately misrepresenting here or whether he was misled by someone else. Obviously we must assume that the iron material of the cuirass was not weighed separately or, at least, that the weight was not exactly checked. We do, however, know that at that time, in contrast to the old Roman ways, the armour of the more distinguished army corps was overlaid with silver (cf. my remarks on the subject in *Acta Arch.* v, 1934, 99), and it is certain that in view of the corruption of the age it was very necessary to control the consumption of this precious metal. We have one exact record of such control: on a helmet of this period ornamented with an overlay of silver, beside the name of the corps, the weight of the silver is inscribed (found in Deurne, Holland; cf. M. A. Evelein in *Prähist. Zeitschr.* iii, 1911, 144 ff.).

18 (p. 48). The ancient sources are collected in Seeck, *Gesch. d. Unt. d. ant. Welt*, v (p. 32, ll. 18 ff.). For the archaeological evidence see, for example, the references to literature in A. Nagl, *RE.* vii A. 2175 and 2182 ff. For the more important details cf.: G. Bersu, *Das römische Kastell in Altrip* (Pfälzisches Museum, 1928, 3); W. Unverzagt, *Germania*, xiii, 1929, 187 ff.; ibid. xvii, 1933, 31 ff.; W. Unverzagt–E. Anthes, *Bonner Jahrb.* cxxii, 1912, 137 ff.; E. Anthes, *10. Bericht d. röm.-germ. Komm.*, 1918, 109 ff.; K. Schumacher, *Siedlungs- und Kulturgesch. d. Rheinlande*, ii, 1923, 339 (lit.); L. Schmidt, *Gesch. d. deutschen Stämme, Die Westgermanen*, ii. 273; K. Stade, *Germania*, xvii, 1933, 31 ff.; F. Kutsch, *Festschr. f. A. Oxé*, 1938, 204–6; W. Schleiermacher, *Germania*, xxvi, 1942, 191 ff.; H. Nesselhauf, *Die spätröm. Verwaltung der gallisch-germanischen Länder*, 1938, 14, 16, 31 ff., 59, 64, 76, 98; F. Stähelin, *Die Schweiz in röm. Zeit³*, 1948, 294 ff.; E. Nowotny, *Römerspuren nördlich der Donau* (Sitz.-Ber. d. Wiener Akad. clxxxiv. 2. Abh.), 1918; E. Nischer-Falkenhof, *Unsere Heimat*, N.F. v, 1932, 227 ff.; A. Alföldi, *Der Untergang der Römerherrschaft in Pannonien*, 1, 1924, 81 ff.; J. Szilágyi, *Inscr. tegul. Pann.* (Diss. Pann. ii. 1, 1933); id., *Archaeológiai Értesítő*, 1941, 60 f.; J. Paulovics, *Arch. Ért.* 1934, 158 ff.; L. Nagy, *Tanulmányok Budapest multjából*, iii, 1934, 3 ff.; &c.

19 (p. 49). Ammianus xxvi. 5. 13: 'tandem denique utilitate rei perpensius

cogitata, in multorum sententias flexus, replicabat aliquotiens, hostem suum fratrisque solius esse Procopium, Alamannos vere totius orbis Romani; statuitque nusquam interim extra confinia moveri Gallorum'. The following passage is taken from a panegyric, delivered by Symmachus (*or.* i. 17–21) 25 February A.D. 369, who varies the theme in detail: 'et tu quidem bellico intentus operi dudum ferocis Alamanniae terga vertebas, sed parte alia fraterni imperii liberam pacem rebellis exul inruperat. quod cum ad te primum pernices nuntii et fidae litterae pertulerunt, quis non congruum iudicavit, ut a caede barbarica in facinus civile arma torqueres? at tu rei publicae plus timebas et inter duas causas hinc intestinam, inde finitimam malebas potentiam tuam interim frui aemulum quam longam impunitatem vicinum. . . . hic communis hostis est [so he makes Valentinian say] ille privatus; prima victoriae publicae, secunda vindictae meae causa est', &c.

20 (p. 51) Ammianus xxvii. 9. 4: 'et quoniam adest liber locus dicendi quae sentimus, aperte loquemur: hunc imperatorem omnium primum, in maius militares fastus ad damna rerum auxisse communium, dignitates opesque eorum sublimius erigentem, . . . qui ex eo anhelantes, ex nutu suo indistanter putant omnium pendere fortunas'. The *omnium primus* is, of course, a mechanical application of the *inventor* motif; actually, the comment might have been more properly made of Septimius Severus, almost 200 years earlier. I have omitted the lines in which Ammianus charges Valentinian with reserving his bloody vengeance for the *gregariorum errata*, but being indulgent to the *potiores*. We have already seen that this was not really so.

21 (p. 51). Ammianus xxx. 8. 10: 'invidia praeter haec ante dictus medullitus urebatur. . . . utque sunt dignitatum apices maximi, licere sibi cuncta existimantes, et ad suspicandum contrarios, exturbandosque meliores, pronius inclinati, bene vestitos oderat et eruditos et opulentos et nobiles, et fortibus detrahebat, ut solus videretur bonis artibus eminere, quo vitio exarsisse principem legimus Hadrianum'. That Ammianus here is acting as interpreter to the feelings of the aristocracy of the City of Rome was recognized by W. Ensslin, *Zur Geschichtesschreibung u. Weltanschauung d. A. M.* 28 ff. It is interesting to observe the connexion of this passage in Ammianus with Zosimus iv. 16. 2, according to which Valentinian τοῖς τε ἐκ τοῦ ζῆν ἀμέμπτως ἔχουσι δόξαν ἐφθόνει κτλ.

22 (p. 54). This follows, for example, from *Epit. de Caes.* 45. 6: 'si ei (Valentiniano) foedis hominibus, quibus sese quasi fidissimis prudentissimisque dederat' (these *foedi homines* are, of course, the Pannonians and their comrades), 'carere, aut probatis eruditisque monitoribus' (these *eruditi* and *probati*, on the other hand, must be the senators) 'uti licuisset, perfectus haud dubie princeps enituisset'. Ammianus shares this view. He writes, for example, of Maximinus (xxviii. 1. 10): 'relatione maligna docuit principem, non nisi suppliciis acrioribus perniciosa facinora scrutari posse vel vindicari'. Again, in the same passage (1. 21): 'haec Valentinianus relatione iudicum doctus, asperius interpretantium facta'; 1. 51: 'haec . . . malignius ad principem Simplicius rettulit, agensque ibi Maximinus infestus . . . Aginatio (oravit) inpense ut rescriberetur eum occidi: et impetravit facile male sanus incitator

et potens' (cf. xxviii. 1. 36–7). Again, according to xxviii. 1. 43, Maximinus as *praefectus praetorio Galliarum* is all-powerful at the Emperor's Court in Gaul and, therefore, the affairs are managed by the *vicarii urbis* as he pleases; cf. 40. 44, xxix. 3. 1 ff.: 'Maximinum . . . iam praefectum, qui potestate late diffusa, scaevum imperatori accesserat incentivum, maiestati fortunae miscenti licentiam gravem . . . aduliscente enim acerbitate, rationum inimica rectarum, trux suopte ingenio Valentinianus, post eiusdem Maximini adventum, nec meliora monente ullo nec retentante, per asperos actus velut aestu quodam fluctuum ferebatur et procellarum . . . . '. Then follow colourful examples to prove that Maximinus was the evil genius of the Emperor. Cf. also xxx. 5. 10: 'urente irarum nutrimenta tunc officiorum magistro Leone.' A. Nagl (*RE*. vii A. 2191) is in error in maintaining that the aristocracy of Rome was almost completely excluded from service at Court: Ausonius, whom we have mentioned, does not come into the question, but, besides Symmachus (and Petronius Probus) we might adduce the *praefectus praetorio* Vulcacius Rufinus, the *vicarius urbis* Anicius Aginatius, and many others; only in comparison with earlier times is there a sharp decline in numbers.

23 (p. 60). *Cod. Theod.* xiv. 17. 5 (1 August A.D. 369): 'idem A.A.A. ad populum. civis Romanus, qui in viginti panibus sordidis, qui nunc dicuntur ardinienses, quinquaginta uncias comparabat, triginta et sex uncias in buccellis sex mundis sine pretio consequatur, ita ut ius in his nullus habeat officialis, nullus servus, nemo qui aedificiorum percipiat panem. quorum siquis se aliqua ratione fortasse inmerserit, adquisito pane privabitur proprium nihilo minus perditurus aut dabit pro condicione supplicium, eo, qui commissam detulit fraudem, et emptoris panes et venditoris habituro. popularibus enim, quibus non est aliunde solacium, quibus idem panis hodieque distrahitur, et eorum successoribus clementia nostra deputavit in quo nunc emitur loco propriis gradibus erogandum. quibus titulus figendus est aeneus, in quem et panis modus et percipientis nomen debebit incidi. et si ad tantum alicuius temeritas eruperit, ut aut per se aut per aliquem suorum sibi quolibet modo ius panis istius aeneae tabulae suum voluerit nomen inserere, supra dictis condicionibus subiacebit. p(ro) p(osita) Romae, Kal. Aug. Val(entini)ano n.p. et Victore conss.' See also the note of Gothofredus on the passage.

24 (p. 64). *Cod. Theod.* xiv. 17. 6: 'idem A.A.A. ad Maximum p.f. ann. Si quis umquam actor, procurator servusque senatoris usurpatum gradilem, gratificante aut vendente scriba vel etiam consentiente, perceperit, subiciatur eculei quaestioni. ac si eundem patuerit temeritate propria adque ignorante domino de perceptione panis inlicite transegisse, ipse sub vinculis pistrino quod fraudabat inserviat; si vero senatoris culpa id fuisse constiterit, domus eius fisci facultatibus adgregetur. ex aliis quoque si quis rei familiaris facultatibus praeditus designatum crimen admiserit, cum his quae habet pistrini exercitio subiugetur. si quis etiam pauperrimus rerum erit, cogetur exhibere operariam servitutem. in scribas vero, quos constiterit nefas vetitum perpetrasse, vindex legum gladius exeratur.'

25 (p. 72). Ammianus xxviii. 1. 30: 'opportunum est (ut arbitror) explanare

nunc causam, quae ad exitium praecipitem Aginatium inpulit, iam inde a priscis maioribus nobilem, ut locuta est pertinacior fama; nec enim super hoc ulla documentorum rata est fides'. The lack of evidence does not refer, of course, to his descent, as W. Ensslin, (*Zur Geschichtsschreibung und Weltanschauung des Ammianus*, 1923, 29) supposes; for in other places Ammianus uses of Aginatius the expressions *homo patriciae stirpis* (ibid. 52), *senator perspicui generis* (ibid. 54); he can have had no doubt, then, about his noble descent. O. Seeck is certainly right in thinking that he belonged to the mighty *gens* of the Anicii (*RE*. i. 809 ff.); the lack of the *documentorum fides* can only refer to the *causa*.

26 (p. 74). Ammianus xxviii. 1. 54–6 (the inquiry by Doryphorianus): 'festinavit (ut mandatum est) Doryphorianus magnis itineribus Romam et inter ⟨odor⟩andi initia magna quaeritabat industria, qua vi senatorem perspicui generis interficeret, iuvantibus nullis. cognitoque eum iam pridem repertum in villa propria custodiri, ipse tamquam capita sontium ⟨Aginatium, pari⟩terque Anepsiam, horrore medio tenebrarum, audire disposuit, quo tempore hebetari solent obstrictae terroribus mentes: ut inter innumera multa, Aiax quoque Homericus docet, optans perire potius luce, quam pati formidinis augmenta nocturnae'; 55: 'et quoniam iudex, quin immo praedo nefandus, ad id solum quod promisit, intentus, cuncta extollebat in maius, iusso sub ⟨quaestione⟩ Aginatio statui, agmina fecit introire carnificum, catenisque sonantibus triste, mancipia squalore diuturno marcentia, in domini caput ad usque ultimum lacerabat exitium, quod in stupri quaestione fieri vetuere clementissimae leges. denique cum iam contigua morti tormenta ancillae voces expressissent obliquas, indicii fide parum plene discussa, Aginatius ad supplicium duci pronuntiatur abrupte, nec auditus cum magnis clamoribus appellaret nomina principum, sublimis raptus occiditur, pari sententia Anepsia interfecta. haec agitante (cum adesset) perque emissarios (cum procul ageret) Maximino, funera urbs deploravit aeterna.'

27 (p. 76). Ammianus xxviii. 1. 10–11: 'cumque multiformiter quasi in proludiis negotium spectaretur, et quidam sulcatis lateribus, nominassent nobiles aliquos tamquam usos artificibus laedendi per clientes aliosque humiles, notos reos et indices, supra plantam (ut dicitur) evagatus, tartareus cognitor, relatione maligna, docuit principem nonnisi suppliciis acrioribus perniciosa facinora scrutari posse vel vindicari, quae Romae perpetravere conplures. his ille cognitis, efferatus, ut erat vitiorum inimicus acer magis quam severus, uno proloquio, in huius modi causas, quas adroganter proposito maiestatis imminutae miscebat, omnes quos iuris prisci iustitia, divorumque arbitria, quaestionibus exemere cruentis, si postulasset negotium, statuit tormentis adfligi'.

28 (p. 77). In the corresponding prosecution of forbidden magic rites in the East our historian is also shocked by the rough handling of the aristocracy. Ammianus xxix. 1. 5 ff.: the prosecutor, Palladius, is *obscurissime natus* (1. 5): the chief of the accused, Theodorus, *antiquitus claro genere natus* (1. 8); of others we read: 'Diogenes . . . vir nobili prosapia editus' (1. 43); 'Alypius ex vicario Britanniarum' (1. 44); 'Bassianus, praeclaro genere natus'

(2. 5). A villainous accuser 'praecipiti confidentia patriciatus columina ipse pulsavit' (2. 9); cf. ibid. 2. 16–17. The confidant of Maximinus, 'Festus proconsul Asiae ultimi sanguinis et ignoti' (xxix. 2. 22).

29 (p. 78). *Cod. Theod.* ix. 16. 10: 'ad Ampelium praefectum urbi: quia nonnulli ex ordine senatorio maleficiorum insimulatione adque invidia stringebantur, idcirco huiusmodi negotia urbanae praefecturae discutienda permisimus. quod si quando huius modi inciderit quaestio, quae iudicio memoratae sedis dirimi vel terminari posse non creditur, eos, quos negotii textus amplectitur, una cum gestis omnibus praesentibus adque praeteritis ad comitatum mansuetudinis nostrae sollemni observatione transmitti praecipimus.' Cf. O. Seeck's comments, trying to connect this constitution with *Cod. Iust.* i. 28. 2 (*Reg.* 123).

30 (p. 79). Ammianus xxviii. 1. 48–9: 'Eumenius enim et Abienus, ambo ex coetu amplissimo, infamati sunt sub Maximino in Fausianam, . . . Simplicii adventu perterrefacti, . . . ad secreta receptacula se contulerunt. sed Fausiana damnata, inter reos recepti, vocatique edictis, semet abstrusius amendarunt', &c. Hieron. *Chron.* p. 246. 10 Helm: 'presbyter Sirmii iniquissime decollatur, quod Octavianum ex proconsule aput se latitantem prodere noluisset'. *Cod. Theod.* ix. 29. 1 (23 March A.D. 374): 'impp. Valentinanus Valens et Gratianus A.A.A. Simplicio vicario. eos, qui secum alicui criminis reos occulendo sociarunt, par atque ipsos reos poena expectet. proposita Romae X. Kal. April. Gratiano A. III et Equitio v. c. conss.' (Cf. the note of Gothofredus on the passage.)

31 (p. 80). Symm. *or.* 4. 9 (p. 334 Seeck): 'quantum est, . . . quod totus senatus non refertur in numerum noxiorum?'; ibid. *epist.* x. 2. 2–3 (p. 277 Seeck): 'minimum restitit, quin omnes occumberemus, tantum flagitii dissignaverant, qui amplissimas potestates malis artibus possidebant. ferox ille Maximinus ob res secundas, incubator iudiciorum, difficilis decidendis simultatibus, promptus ineundis, poena capitali exitia cunctorum lacrimasque expiavit. nunc interlucet homo homini, senatus ius antiquum obtinet, . . . nulli a paupertate discrimen est.' There is a very interesting passage in the works of Symmachus on the sins of the régime of Maximinus. As its rhetorical *mise-en-scène* is exactly that of Ammianus, this conformity of style must have been in their common source, in the *Annals* of Nicomachus too. The passage is in *or.* iv. 13–14: 'nullae iam nuptiae caesa parente iunguntur nec funeri succedit hymenaeus neque flammeo vestis atra mutatur. credetne posteritas, olim talia fuisse iudicia, quae conubia satellitum suorum sacrarent auspice pugione, spineam facem de rogo damnatae matris incenderent, ululatibus adultarum carmina fescennina miscerent? quid loquar crimina necdum delata iam vendita et humani sanguinis auctiones, aut eruditos in mendacium reos et subornandi artifices ianitores, veteres calumnias novas poenas, crimina sine accusatore, iudicia sine iure, sine iure sententias? . . . rerum versa condicio est: paulo ante soli invidiam felicitatis trahebant, quos mors subripuit istis aerumnis, miserabiles nunc habentur, quos vita non servavit his gaudiis.'

32 (p. 81). In the letter of the Council of A.D. 378 (Mansi iii. 624): 'sic

denique factio profecit Ursino, ut Isaac Iudaeo subornato ... sancti fratris nostri Damasi caput peteretur'; Rufin. *H.E.* ii. 10 (p. 1018 Mommsen), on the quarrel between Damasus and Ursinus: 'quo ex facto tanta seditio, immo vero bella tanta coorta sunt, alterutrum defendentibus populis, ut replerentur humano sanguine orationum loca. quae res factione Maximini praefecti, saevi hominis, ad invidiam boni et innocentis versa est sacerdotis, ita ut causa ad clericorum usque tormenta deduceretur. sed assertor innocentiae deus affuit et in caput eorum qui intenderant dolum poena conversa est'; Socrat. *H.E. 4.* 29: καὶ διὰ τοῦτο πολλοὺς λαϊκούς τε καὶ κληρικοὺς ὑπὸ τοῦ τότε ἐπάρχου Μαξιμίνου τιμωρηθῆναι καὶ οὕτω τόν τε Οὐρσῖνον παύσασθαι τῆς ἐπιχειρήσεως καὶ κατασταλῆναι τοὺς βουληθέντας ἀκολουθῆσαι αὐτῷ. (In shorter form, Sozom. 6. 23.) Cf. also E. Caspar, *Zeitschr. f. Kirchengesch.* xlvii, 1928, 185 ff. and the same in *Gesch. d. Papsttums,* i, 1930, 200 ff.

33 (p. 82). J. Wittig, 'Die Friedenspolitik des Papstes Damasus I' (*Kirchengesch. Abh. v. Sdralek,* x, 1912, 69 ff.) calls attention to the part played by the orthodox presbyter of Antioch, Euagrius, who vigorously supported the cause of Damasus before Valentinian (cf. also E. Caspar, op. cit. 204. 7). It is based on Jerome, *ep.* 1. 15 (*Corp. Script. Eccl. Lat.* liv. 8): 'ad Evagrii nostri nomen advenimus. cuius ego pro Christo laborem, si arbitrer a me dici posse, non sapiam; si penitus tacere velim, voce in gaudium erumpente non possim. quis enim valeat digno canere praeconio, Auxentium Mediolani incubantem huius excubiis sepultum paene antequam mortuum, Romanum episcopum iam paene factionis laqueis irretitum et vicisse adversarios et non nocuisse superatis?'

34 (p. 83). The party of Ursinus jeered at Damasus, calling him the 'matrons' ear-scratcher' (*epist. imper.* 1, c. 9 f. (*Corp. Script. Eccl. Lat.* xxxv. 4): 'quem in tantum matronae diligebant, ut matronarum auriscalpius diceretur'). Ammianus writes of the quarrel between Damasus and Ursinus in the following terms (xxvii. 3. 14): 'neque ego abnuo, ostentationem rerum considerans urbanarum, huius rei cupidos ob impetrandum quod appetunt, omni contentione laterum iurgare debere, cum id adepti, futuri sint ita securi, ut ditentur oblationibus matronarum, procedantque vehiculis insidentes, circumspecte vestiti, epulas curantes profusas, adeo ut eorum convivia regales superent mensas'. Cf. E. Caspar, *Zeitschr. f. Kirchengesch.* xlvii, 1928, 186.

35 (p. 83). *Cod. Theod.* xvi. 2. 20: 'impp. Val(entini)anus Valens et Gratianus A.A.A. ad Damasum episc(opum) urbis Rom(ae). ecclesiastici aut ex ecclesiasticis vel qui continentium volunt se nomine nuncupari, viduarum ac pupillarum domos non adeant, sed publicis exterminentur iudiciis, si posthac eos adfines earum vel propinqui putaverint deferendos. censemus etiam, ut memorati nihil de eius mulieris, cui se privatim sub praetextu religionis adiunxerint, liberalitate quacumque vel extremo iudicio possint adipisci et omne in tantum inefficax sit, quod alicui horum ab his fuerit derelictum, ut nec per subiectam personam valeant aliquid vel donatione vel testamento percipere. quin etiam, si forte post admonitionem legis nostrae aliquid isdem eae feminae vel donatione vel extremo iudicio putaverint

relinquendum, id fiscus usurpet. ceterum si earum quid voluntate percipiunt, ad quarum successionem vel bona iure civili vel edicti beneficiis adiuvantur, capiant ut propinqui. lecta in ecclesiis Rom(ae) III. Kal. Aug. Val(entini)ano et Valente III A.A. conss.'

36 (p. 87). Symm. *or.* 5. 3: 'ad te etiam, venerabilis imperator, laudis istius summa referenda est. is enim rem publicam liberam tenet, sub quo aliquid invidendum in potestate senatus. ideo magnus, ideo praeclarus es, quia primum te mavis esse quam solum. quidquid adipiscuntur boni, saeculo tuo proficit. traxerunt olim plerique ⟨principum in invidiam, si quisquam absens civium moveret⟩ suspiria et quasi amari imperatoribus tantum liceret, privatorum merita presserunt. mihi autem vere pater patriae videtur, sub quo laudari vir optimus non timet. est etiam illa securitas temporis tui, quod nemo se apud principem minorem fieri putat, si ipse alterum sibi praeferat. quis enim est invidiae locus cum omnes a te iusto ordine diligantur?'

37 (p. 89). *Cod. Theod.* ix. 1. 13 (11 February A.D. 376), a law addressed to the Senate: 'provincialis iudex vel intra Italiam, cum in eius disceptationem criminalis causae dictio adversum senatorem inciderit, intendendi quidem examinis et cognoscendi causas habeat potestatem, verum nihil de animadversione decerno. integro non causae sed capitis statu referat ad scientiam nostram vel ad inclytas potestates. referant igitur praesides et correctores, item consulares, vicarii quoque, proconsules de capite, ut diximus, senatorio negotii examine habito. Referant autem de suburbanis provinciis iudices ad praefecturam sedis urbanae, de ceteris ad praefecturam praetorio. sed praefecto urbis cognoscenti de capite senatorum spectatorum maxime virorum iudicium quinquevirale sociabitur et de praesentibus et administratorum honore functis licebit adiungere sorte ductos, non sponte electos.' Cf. Ch. H. Coster, *The 'iudicium quinquevirale'* (Acad. Monogr. Cambr., Mass.), 1935.

38 (p. 92). Symm. *or.* 4. 10: 'at primo consilium tuum deliberatio distulit, dum experiris, an improbi atque externi mores exemplo saeculi vincerentur, vel quod optimo filio congruebat, dum palam facere studes praeterita delicta potestatum fuisse non temporum. sciebas enim, quo spectaret invidia, cui familiare est maximas insimulare fortunas, adque ideo paulisper inpotentiam passus es, ut liqueret, eos publici doloris auctores dudum fuisse, qui etiam tum nocendi artem colebant, cum iam noverant non licere'. The last expression is a nasty hit at the dead Emperor: till then it had been allowed *nocendi artem colere.*

39 (p. 92). Symm. *or.* 4. 11–12: 'interea nos opperiebamur, ut principatus ultro talia vindicaret, vos exspectabatis, ut senatus argueret. credo tamen, has moras ad suffragium publicae causae parasse fortunam, ut suscepturus, Gratiane venerabilis, iudicium doloris nostri, adferres testimonium tui; etsi illud magis confirmare me convenit, nostram legationem nostras egisse querimonias, ut videreris tu quoque inter ceteros vindicari. nam priusquam senatus causa iungeretur tuae, satisfactum tibi putabas, quod insidiator regni exemplo innocentium potestate decesserat; postquam ventum est ad communes querellas, adhibuisti severitatem, qualem reliqui principes

maiestatis tantum negotiis exhibebant. actum erat, clementissime imperator, de iniuria tua, nisi nobilitas fuisset offensa.'

40 (p. 93). Symmachus simply ignored the fact that he had recently been praising Valentinian (*ep.* x. 1. 2: 'laus temporum'), while abusing Maximinus, after his execution (*ep.* x. 2. 2–3). The courtesy due to Gratian binds him, but only ends in making him somewhat lukewarm in his defence of Gratian's father, by making his entourage responsible for his unpopularity; *or.* 4. 9: 'etiam famam saeculi superioris diligentiores posteri diluerunt. neque enim fas est negari, non alios divum principem pertulisse hostes existimationis, quam nos salutis. iamne constat fortunam nobilitatis consentire temporibus? eadem iustitia purgavit imperium quae senatum'; *or.* 4. 10: 'gratulamur tibi, iuvenis Auguste, quod paterni successor factus imperii, tantum malos iudices quasi hereditatis onera repudiasti. non satis tibi idonea bona illa visa sunt cum ⟨malorum⟩ ministris'.

41 (p. 93). Symm. *or.* 4. 4: 'ubi sunt, qui falso animis inbiberunt, magis efficacem esse audaciam factionis quam voluntates bonorum? nempe fugit repulsa virtutem et contra ambitus omnis ignavus est. quod honeste poscitur, feliciter impetratur. hoc ius patriciae genti tempora (sc. Gratiani) reddiderunt; postulatio (sc. consulatus ab imperatore) vestra iudicium est.' Ibid. 15: 'vellem nunc truces iudices sciscitari, quae validior emendatio sit? olim timor agebat, ut bonus quisque trepidaret, nunc honor facit, ut malus quisque desperet'. On similar outbreaks in *or.* 5. 5 see Seeck, *Symm.* prol., pp. vi, lii.

42 (p. 93). Symm. *or.* 4. 5: 'quam raro huic rei publicae, patres conscripti, tales principes contigerunt, qui idem vellent, idem statuerent, quod senatus! nemo olim sibi in illa arce fortunae potens nimium videbatur, nisi diversa sensisset. quantis plerumque offuit amor publicus! neque enim pati poterat sollicitudo domini cuiquam deferri, quod ipse non merebatur. impatiens est alienae gratiae, qui diffidit suae. hinc saepe mortalium pessimos ad amplissimas potestates fatorum volatus evexit, scilicet hoc uno placendi suffragio, quia omnibus displicebant. genus quoddam erat novi ambitus non amari. hanc illecebram propositae spei mores sequebantur; ita accidebat, ut boni, quibus adversa omnia erant, aut opprimerentur improborum insidiis aut mutarentur exemplis' (is he thinking of Probus here?); ibid. 6: 'at nunc idem principes nostri quod proceres volunt. unum corpus est rei publicae adque ideo maxime viget, quia capitis robusta sanitas valetudinem membrorum tuetur. amor vester praerogativa est consulatus; magistratus boni capiunt, quia non ab uno tantum sed ab omnibus eliguntur. sciunt enim parentes generis humani diligentiora iudicia esse multorum.'

43 (p. 94). Symmachus (*ep.* x. 2. 1) wishes to emphasize the magnitude of the distinction that Gratian has conferred on him in asking him to read this important expression of his will: 'non idem honor in pronuntiandis fabulis Publilio Pellioni qui Ambivio fuit, neque par Aesopo et Roscio fama processit'; ibid. 5: 'igitur divina mens tua, iuvenis Auguste, Romani nominis decus, vehatur curru eloquii sui: nos in agendis gratiis humile reptamus, socco magis idonei quam cothurno, postquam facundia res esse coepit

imperii: nam quod sciam, Musis in palatio loca lautia tu dedisti. quae res prospere vortat vobis vestraeque pietati'.

44 (p. 100). Victor, *Caes.* 25. 1–2: 'namque Gaius Iulius Maximinus . . ., primus a militaribus, litterarum fere rudis potentiam cepit suffragiis legionum. quod tamen etiam patres, dum periculosum existimant inermes armato resistere, approbaverunt'; Eutropius 9. 1: 'post hunc Maximinus ex corpore militari primus ad imperium accessit sola militum voluntate, cum nulla senatus intercessisset auctoritas, neque ipse senator esset'; Script. hist. Aug., *Maximini duo* 8. 1: 'sed occiso Alexandro Maximinus primum e corpore militari et nondum senator sine decreto senatus Augustus ab exercitu appellatus est'; Hieron. *Chron.* a. 236 (p. 216 D Helm): 'Maximinus primus ex corpore militari sine senatus auctoritate ab exercitu imperator electus est'. These agreements show that the idea goes back to the 'Anonymus' of Enmann. See the study of my much regretted friend G. M. Bersanetti, *Studi sull' imperatore Maximino il Trace*, 1940, 9 ff.; F. Altheim, *Die Krise der alten Welt*, iii, 1943, 221, no. 92; W. Ensslin, *Rhein. Mus.* xc. 1 ff.; E. Hohl, *Klio*, xxxiv, 1942, 264 ff.; *Rhein. Mus.* xci. 164 ff.; F. Altheim, ibid. 350 ff. Lastly cf. W. Hartke, in *Maximini duo*, ed. E. Hohl (Kleine Texte No. 172, 1949), 8.

45 (p. 100). Victor, *Caes.* 24. 8–11: 'quae (respublica) iam tum a Romulo ad Septimium certatim evolans Bassiani consiliis tamquam in summo constitit. quo ne confestim laberetur Alexandri fuit. abhinc dum dominandi suis quam subigendi externos cupientiores sunt atque inter se armantur magis, Romanum statum quasi abrupto praecipitavere, inmissique in imperium promiscue boni malique, nobiles atque ignobiles, ac barbariae multi. quippe ubi passim confusaque omnia neque suo feruntur modo, quique fas putant, uti per turbam, rapere aliena officia, quae regere nequeunt, et scientiam bonarum artium foede corrumpunt. ita fortunae vis licentiam nacta perniciosa libidine mortales agit: quae diu quidem virtute uti muro prohibita, postquam paene omnes flagitiis subacti sunt, etiam infimis genere institutoque publica permisit.'

46 (p. 100). Victor, *Caes.* 36. 1: 'igitur tandem senatus . . . Tacitum e consularibus . . . imperatorem creat, cunctis fere laetioribus, quod militari ferocia legendi ius principis proceres recepissent'; 37. 5–7 (after the death of Probus): 'abhinc militaris potentia convaluit ac senatui imperium creandique ius principis ereptum ad nostram memoriam, incertum an ipso cupiente per desidiam, an metu seu dissensionum odio. quippe amissa Gallieni edicto refici militia potuit concedentibus modeste legionibus Tacito regnante, neque Florianus temere invasisset, aut iudicio manipularium cuiquam, bono licet, imperium daretur, amplissimo ac tanto ordine in castris degente. verum dum oblectantur otio simulque divitiis pavent, quarum usum affluentiamque aeternitate maius putant, munivere militaribus et paene barbaris viam in se ac posteros dominandi.'

47 (p. 102). The compiler of the *Historia Augusta*, in his biography, constructs out of the statement in Herodian a mixed Gothic and Alan origin for Maximin; this is obviously a perversion of the truth. See F. Altheim, *Die*

Soldatenkaiser, 1939, 245 ff., and further *Rhein. Mus.* xc, 1941, 192 ff., and *Die Krise der alten Welt*, iii, 1943, 115 ff. Against his views see my comments in *Századok*, lxxiv, 1940, 429 ff.; W. Hartke, *Klio* (Beih. xlv), 1940, 167, n. 4; W. Ensslin, *Rhein. Mus.* xci, 1942, 164 ff.; M. Bersanetti, *Studi sull'imperatore Massimino il Trace*, 1940, 73 ff., and E. Hohl, *Klio*, xxxiv, 1942, 264 ff. What Herodian means by 'barbarian' is best grasped in his account of the murder of Maximinus Thrax, viii. 6. 1: καὶ οὐ πάνυ τι τῷ πραχθέντι πάντες ἠρέσκοντο, καὶ μάλιστά γε οἱ Παίονες καὶ ὅσοι βάρβαροι Θρᾷκες, οἳ τὴν ἀρχὴν αὐτῷ ἐνεκεχειρίκεσαν.

48 (p. 103). Mamertinus, *Grat. act. Iuliano* 25. 1–2: 'habuerunt nonnulli alii principes devotam et amantem sui cohortem, sed alio quodam modo; primum quod imperiti ac rudes indoctissimum quemque in consilium delegebant, scilicet ut ipsorum prudentia vulgo suorum aliquatenus emineret. ita, cum vilissimus quisque honorum et divitiarum potitus foret, sua commoda et vitia principum diligebant. ab his optimus quisque abigebatur procul, cum suspecta esset probitas et invisa, et quanto quisque honestior tanto importunior turpium arbiter vitaretur.' This confusion of primitive conditions and corruption is malicious; it is a pity that Mamertinus should have descended to it: see on him H. Gutzwiller, *Die Neujahrsrede des Konsuls Claudius Mamertinus vor dem Kaiser Julian* (Basler Beitr. z. Geschichtswiss. x, 1942).

49 (p. 107). Eumenius, *Pro instaurandis scholis*, 5. 3–4, on the Lords of the Tetrarchy: 'et inter illas imperatorias dispositiones, longe maioribus summae rei publicae gubernandae provisionibus occupatas, litterarum quoque habuere dilectum neque aliter quam si equestri turmae vel cohorti praetoriae consulendum foret, quem potissimum praeficerent sui arbitrii esse duxerunt, ne hi quos ad spem omnium tribunalium aut interdum ad stipendia cognitionum sacrarum aut fortasse ad ipsa palatii magisteria provehi oporteret, veluti repentino nubilo in mediis adulescentiae fluctibus deprehensi, incerta dicendi signa sequerentur'. Cf. E. P. Parks, *The Roman Rhetorical Schools as a preparation for the Courts under the Early Empire*, Baltimore, 1945; Ch. Lécrivain, 'Note sur le recrutement des avocats dans la période du Bas-Empire' (*Mél. d'Archéol. et d'Hist.* v, 1885, 276 ff.); M. Conrat, in *Mél. Fitting*, i, 1907; Ét. Collinet, *Histoire de l'École de Droit de Beyrouth*, 1925, passim.

50 (p. 108). Greg. Naz. *or.* 4. 43; 5. 19. Mamertinus, *Grat. act.* 25. 1 ff. is only using the familiar antithetic figures of the panegyric when he maintains that, hitherto, 'imperiti ac rudes' Emperors 'indoctissimum quemque in consilium delegebant', whilst now (25. 3): 'at tu, Auguste, ... optimum ac doctissimum quemque perquiris ...; qui in oratoria facultate, qui in scientia iuris civilis excellit, ultro ad familiaritatem vocatur'. This ideal of the late aristocracy is reflected in the idealized picture of the pagan Emperor, in the compiler of the *Historia Augusta*. Cf. *Alex. Sev.* 16. 3: 'fuit praeterea illi consuetudo, ut, si de iure aut de negotiis tractaret, solos doctos et disertos adhiberet, si vero de re militari, milites veteres ...; et omnes litteratos et maxime eos, qui historiam norant, perquirens, quid in talibus causis, quales in disceptatione versabantur, veteres imperatores vel Romani vel exterarum gentium fecissent'.

51 (p. 108). *Incerti paneg. Constantino Aug. dictus*, 23. 1–2: 'interim quoniam ad summam votorum meorum tua dignatione perveni, ut haec meam qualemcumque vocem diversis otii et palatii officiis exercitam in tuis auribus consecrarem, maximas numini tuo gratias ago tibique . . . commendo liberos meos praecipueque illum iam summa fisci patrocinia tractantem. . . . ceterum quod de omnibus liberis dixi, lata est, imperator, ambitio. praeter illos enim quinque quos genui etiam illos quasi meos numero quos provexi ad tutelam fori, ad officia palatii. multi quippe ex me rivi non ignobiles fluunt, multi sectatores mei etiam provincias tuas administrant.'

52 (p. 109). Themist. p. 22. 4 Dind.: ἤγαγε τοίνυν Θεμίστιον τὸν φιλόσοφον εἰς τὰς ἡμετέρας ἀκοὰς ἡ πολυθρύλητος δόξα, καὶ βασιλικῆς ὑπέλαβον καὶ τῆς ὑμετέρας διανοίας ἀμείψασθαι τιμῇ τῇ προσηκούσῃ τὴν ἀρετήν, τῇ συνόδῳ τῶν λαμπροτάτων πατέρων τὸν ἄνδρα ἐγκαταλέξας τὰ εἰκότα σεμνυνόμενον δι' ἀλλήλων. οὐ γὰρ μόνον Θεμίστιον τιμᾶν οἴομαι διὰ τῆς χάριτος, ἀλλ' οὐδὲν ἧττον καὶ τὴν γερουσίαν, ἣν τὸ μετασχεῖν δωρεᾶς ἄξιον νενόμικα φιλοσοφίᾳ πρεπούσης. διδόντες οὖν ἀντιλήψεσθε τὸν κόσμον καὶ λαμβάνοντες ἀντιδώσετε. ἄλλο μὲν γὰρ ἄλλους κοσμεῖ καὶ περιφανεῖς καθίστησι τοὺς μὲν χρημάτων εὔκλεια τοὺς δὲ κτημάτων περιουσία ἐνίους δὲ πόνοι δημόσιοι ἑτέρους δὲ λόγων δεινότης. διαφόροις γὰρ ὁδοῖς καὶ ποικίλαις πρὸς ἓν καὶ ταὐτὸν ἄκρον τῆς εὐδοξίας ἅπαντες οἱ νοῦν ἔχοντες ἐξαμιλλῶνται. ἀλλ' ὅμως τῶν πολλῶν ἀτραπῶν αἱ μὲν ἄλλαι σκολιαὶ καὶ ἀκροσφαλεῖς, μόνη δὲ ἀσφαλὴς καὶ βέβαιος ἡ δι' ἀρετῆς. καὶ ὅταν τις ὑμῖν ἐγκαταλέγεσθαι μέλλῃ, τοῦτο πρὸ ἁπάντων ζητεῖτε, εἰ ταύτην πορεύεται τὴν πορείαν, καὶ μηδὲν ἄλλο τοιοῦτον γνώρισμα ἡγεῖσθε τῶν λαμπροτάτων ὡς γνώμην ὀρθὴν καὶ διάνοιαν ἀγαθήν, ἃ μάλιστα μεταδιώκει φιλοσοφία.
Ib. p. 23. 16 Dind.: καὶ ὡς μικρὰ ταῦτα λέγω, τὸ δὲ ἀληθὲς κριτὴς ἁπάντων ἐστὶ καὶ ἐπιστάτης ὁ φιλόσοφος. καὶ γὰρ ὅπως δήμῳ προσενεκτέον καὶ ὅπως τὴν γερουσίαν θεραπευτέον καὶ ἁπλῶς ἁπάσης πολιτείας κανών ἐστιν ἐξητασμένος καὶ ἀκριβής, ὡς εἰ δυνατὸν ἦν πᾶσιν ἀνθρώποις φιλοσοφεῖν, ἐξήρπαστο μὲν ἂν ἐκ τοῦ τῶν ἀνθρώπων βίου ἡ φαυλότης, ἐξώριστο δὲ ἅπασα πρόφασις ἀδικίας, τῆς δὲ ἐκ τῶν νόμων ἀνάγκης οὐκ ἂν ἦν χρεία. ὧν γὰρ νῦν διὰ τὸ δέος ἀπέχονται, ταῦτα ἂν ἐμίσουν ἐκ προαιρέσεως.

53 (p. 112). Even Aurelius Victor who, as a man of breeding, is opposed to the rough soldiery, paints with high praise the ideal, so dear to that age, of the martyr for culture (see my remarks in *Die Kontorniaten*, 1943, 78 ff.) when, confusing the Emperor Didius Iulianus with the great jurist Salvius Iulianus (*Caes*. 20. 1 ff.) he writes against Septimius Severus: 'igitur Septimius . . . Salvii nomen atque eius scripta factaque aboleri iubet; quod unum effici nequivit. tantum gratia doctarum artium valet, ut scriptoribus ne saevi mores quidem ad memoriam officiant. quin etiam mors huiuscemodi ipsis gloriae, exsecrationi actoribus est, cum omnes, praecipueque posteri, sic habent, illa ingenia nisi publico latrocinio ac per dementiam opprimi non potuisse.' He goes on to show that he is thinking of the present (20. 5): 'quo bonis omnibus ac mihi fidendum magis . . .'

54 (p. 112). Victor, *Caes*. 8. 7–8: 'hi omnes, quos paucis attigi, praecipueque Caesarum gens adeo litteris culti atque eloquentia fuere, ut, ni cunctis vitiis absque Augusto nimii forent, tantae artes profecto texissent modica

flagitia. quis rebus quamquam satis constet praestare mores, tamen bono cuique, praesertim summo rectori, utroque, si queat, iuxta opus: sin aliter, vitae proposito inmensum regrediente elegantiae saltem atque eruditionis sumat auctoritatem'; *Epit. de Caes.* 8. 6: 'hi omnes, quos paucis attigi, praecipue Caesarum gens, adeo litteris culti atque eloquentia fuere, ut, ni cunctis vitiis absque Augusto nimii forent, profecto texissent modica flagitia'.

55 (p. 112). Victor, *Caes.* 10. 1: 'ceterum Titus, postquam imperium adeptus est, incredibile quantum, quem imitabatur, anteierit, praesertim litteris clementiaque ac muneribus'; *Epit. de Caes.* 13. 7–9: 'de quo supervacaneum videtur cuncta velle nominatim promere, cum satis sit excultum atque emendatum dixisse. 8: . . . Traianus) magis simpliciora ingenia aut eruditissimos, quamvis ipse parcae esset scientiae moderateque eloquens, diligebat'; Eutropius, 8. 7 on Hadrian: 'facundissimus Latino sermone, Graeco eruditissimus fuit'; *Vita Hadr.* 1. 5; 3. 1 (following Marius Maximus); Eutropius 8. 12, on Marcus: 'institutus est ad philosophiam. . . . hic cum omnibus Romae aequo iure egit, ad nullum insolentiam elatus est imperii fastigio'; Victor, *Caes.* 16. 1–2: '. . . (Aurelium Antoninum) . . . philosophandi vero eloquentiaeque studiis longe praestantem, . . . cuius divina omnia domi militiaeque facta consultaque'; ibid. 16. 9–10: 'tantumque Marco sapientiae lenitudinis innocentiae ac litterarum fuisse, ut is Marcomannos . . . petiturus philosophorum turba obtestantium circumfunderetur, ne expeditioni aut pugnae se prius committeret, quam sectarum ardua ac perocculta explanavisset. ita incerta belli in eius salute et doctrinae studiis metuebantur; tantumque illo imperante floruere artes bonae, ut illam gloriam etiam temporum putem'; *Vita Marci* 1. 1: 'Marco Antonino, in omni vita philosophanti viro . . .'; 2. 1 ff. (more details about his education and learning); Victor, *Caes.* 20. 22 (on Severus): 'philosophiae, declamandi, cunctis postremo liberalium deditus studiis; idemque abs se texta ornatu et fide paribus composuit'; *Epit. de Caes.* 20. 8: 'Latinis litteris sufficienter instructus, Graecis sermonibus eruditus, Punica eloquentia promptior quippe genitus apud Leptim provinciae Africae'; Eutropius 8. 19: 'Severus autem praeter bellicam gloriam etiam civilibus studiis clarus fuit et litteris doctus, philosophiae scientiam ad plenum adeptus'; *Epit. de Caes.* 29. 2 (on Decius): 'vir artibus cunctis virtutibusque instructus'.

56 (p. 118). Themist. *or.* 7, p. 118. 25 ff. Dind. (Valens holds philosophy in honour, less so ὑμεῖς οἱ τοῖς ὅπλοις ἐντεθραμμένοι); *or.* 8. p. 135. 25 ff.: οἰκίας πρότερον ἐπεμελήθης ἢ βασιλείας, καὶ μετήνεγκας ἀπὸ τῶν ἐλαττόνων ἐπὶ τὰ μείζω τὴν ἐμπειρίαν . . .· οὐδέν σε δεῖ ζητεῖν τοὺς διδάξοντας ἐξ ὅσων ἱδρώτων περιγίγνεται τοῖς γεωργοῖς καὶ ἡμίεκτον καὶ ἀμφίεκτον καὶ ἀμφορεὺς καὶ χαλκοῦς εἷς καὶ ἀργυροῦς στατὴρ χρυσοῦς τε, ὅτι καὶ θέαμα ἀγαπητὸν τοῖς πολλοῖς ἀνθρώποις . . . ταύτην παιδευθεὶς τὴν παιδείαν ἐπὶ τοῦτο τὸ βῆμα ἀνῆλθες, ἣν ἐπαιδεύθη . . . Νουμᾶς ἐν τοῖς πάλαι Ῥωμαίοις, ὃν ἡ σύγκλητος Ῥωμαίων ἀροῦντα ἐν ἐξωμίδι ἀποσπάσασα τοῦ ζεύγους ἡμφίεσε τῇ ἁλουργίδι.

57 (p. 119). Ammianus xxix. 2. 18: 'o praeclara informatio doctrinarum munere caelesti indulta felicibus, quae vel vitiosas naturas saepe excoluisti! quanta in illa caligine temporum correxisses, si Valenti scire per te licuisset,

nihil aliud esse imperium, ut sapientes definiunt, nisi curam salutis alienae, bonique esse moderatoris, restringere potestatem, resistere cupiditati omnium rerum, et implacabilibus iracundiis, nosseque (ut Caesar dictator aiebat) miserum esse instrumentum senectuti recordationem crudelitatis, ideoque de vita et spiritu hominis, qui pars mundi est et animantium numerum complet, laturam sententiam, diu multumque cunctari oportere, nec praecipiti studio, ubi inrevocabile factum est, agitari, ut exemplum est illud antiquitati admodum notum'.

INDEX